# ATTEMPTING TO Let Go

*Attempting To Let Go by Athena Grace*

*ISBN 978-1-952027-24-6 (Paperback)*
*ISBN 978-1-952027-25-3 (Hardback)*

*This book is written to provide information and motivation to readers. Its purpose is not to render any type of psychological, legal, or professional advice of any kind. The content is the sole opinion and expression of the author, and not necessarily that of the publisher.*

*Copyright © 2025 by Athena Grace*

*All rights reserved. No part of this book may be reproduced, transmitted, or distributed in any form by any means, including, but not limited to, recording, photocopying, or taking screenshots of parts of the book, without prior written permission from the author or the publisher. Brief quotations for noncommercial purposes, such as book reviews, permitted by Fair Use of the U. S. Copyright Law, are allowed without written permissions, as long as such quotations do not cause damage to the book's commercial value. For permissions, write to the publisher, whose address is stated below.*

*Printed in the United States of America*
*New Leaf Media, LLC*
*470 W Broad St #1276*
*Columbus, OH 43215*
*thenewleafmedia.com*

## *Acknowledgements*

I credit everyone in my life who guided me to write these words of wisdom. For, divorce seems to have so many life stages, and they seem to last for years. We do not have a choice on whether we want to deal with it; if only for ourselves and for our kids. However, with each presentation of grief, remorse, and each new trial we must face, we really can deal with it, and then move forward. But we must want to move ahead, for each difficulty we face, there are higher powers that can help us get there. We can then look back and realize that we really can make life more enjoyable because we faced our fears and won. The emptiness we feel afterwards will ultimately subside, but only with help from others and with our determination. Just remember, at this point in life, we have learned a lot from our trials, and we wouldn't be where we are now if we had not faced them and triumphed!

Thanks to everyone who helped me to create this memoir of thoughts and events that have shaped my existence.

# *Dedication*

This book is dedicated to those who gone down the path of "divorce" and have endured. The following chapters will follow men and women after years of tragedy. It will show where they are now in their career, family life, and in their personal life. It will compare lives of men and women who have made choices to pick themselves up, brush off the dust, or "rust" in some cases, and then continue by themselves. Some of the people I have written about have chosen to find that "real" soul mate that they were always meant to be with, and they are currently pursuing that venture.

This book also follows men and women who have been married for years but have only been separated by death. It will show statistics on divorce from our 20s onward, different groups of people who experience divorce, people who never get remarried, and the changes people experience throughout the years.

# Table of Contents

| | | | |
|---|---|---|---|
| **Chapter 1** | - | I Survived, Or Did I? | 01 |
| **Chapter 2** | - | Till Death Due Us Part— Are You Kidding Me? | 16 |
| **Chapter 3** | - | Does Marriage Equal Bliss? | 27 |
| **Chapter 4** | - | If I Can Accomplish It, It Isn't A Problem, Right? | 43 |
| **Chapter 5** | - | Embracing the Storm | 60 |
| **Chapter 6** | - | Hold Me Tight and Make The Pain Go Away | 72 |
| **Chapter 7** | - | The Next Chapter of Me | 86 |
| **Chapter 8** | - | Where Do I Go From Here? | 103 |
| **Chapter 9** | - | After The Death of Divorce | 121 |
| **Chapter 10** | - | Happily Ever After— Whoever Came Up With That Crap? | 136 |
| **Chapter 11** | - | Help Me Understand | 148 |
| **Chapter 12** | - | Destination—"Life" | 163 |
| **Chapter 13** | - | Memories—Happy or Otherwise | 180 |
| **Chapter 14** | - | Can I Order Another Round? | 190 |
| **Chapter 15** | - | I have the aspirin—where's my headache? | 201 |
| **Chapter 16** | - | A Man's Opinion | 209 |
| **Chapter 17** | - | The Sun will Rise Again | 217 |
| **Chapter 18** | - | The Final Chapter—Maybe? | 230 |

## 01.

## *I Survived Or Did I*

Congratulations are now in order! Yes, you've now made it to the top of that mountain called "divorce," and now you're coasting down to the other side. Now, it's time to find our little red wagon to carry out our life's mission. It doesn't seem so hard now since the first year or so has gone by, right? Well duh! That would a major "NO!" You're still a little uncomfortable with dating and being alone in a crowd, but you haven't given up hope that that right person is still out there for you. You've gotten used to paying your own bills, cleaning your own house, figuring out how to fix things, or even hiring someone to fix things that go wrong in your home. But there's still something missing in your life, you can just feel it. You enjoy your free time, and you don't have a significant other who keeps you up at night from their snoring. Plus, now you clean up only after yourself. It's too good to be true, right? Well, maybe.

With everything that is going right in your life now, is there anything going in the totally opposite direction? Well, to start with, you have a hard time trusting what comes out of the mouth of ANY potential partner, you still feel a little inadequate because your ex is still "your ex," and will always be called that, and your mindset has changed. Some of the things you still hear about, what he or she does to and with other people still irritates you. Plus, you're getting into a new routine that just a year or more ago would have made you feel uneasy. Do you ever wonder why getting a headache is so natural now?

So, what are your goals and where is your life taking you? Do you feel you have to be in a relationship with a special someone? Or have you completely and totally decided that being with someone again is absolutely not worth the effort? Whatever your response, your life is now what you can make it. Besides, is your heart ready for love, respect and adoration from a special someone? Moreover, does anyone have these types of feelings stashed somewhere at the bottom of that organ that keeps pumping blood to their very being? I assume that we all now want a certain level of intimacy in our lives, but how far are we willing to go to achieve it? I had a girlfriend tell me last week that after her recent divorce she wanted to get back into the dating world. However, the men she is now meeting are bitter about their past relationships. Have they gone through something worse than all the women out there? Besides, where do we get the "new " mindset to convince us that not everyone is a red-headed, bastard child out to stab us in the back? I'm probably going a little too far with that statement, but don't we all have a little resentment that we can't shake? I thought so.

Now that we've been hurt, humiliated, and we've gone so far to the left side, that the right side doesn't exist anymore, so what's next? Where do we go from here? Our friends, family, and even our boss is scrutinizing our difficult times. I guess how we deal with them is who we become? Is this right or wrong? Who knows? That's debatable because life has a way of making us look at ourselves like we never have before. Think of life this way, if going to church was a priority before we got married, but after the "I Do's," it wasn't in our schedule anymore—what happened to our values? As we built our life together with this person, did we conform to "their" standards, to mesh as a couple, vice our own values? Then, after we parted ways, do we now realize what we once held dear is something we now want back? Or do we look behind us and see that we have changed because of them, and are now sorry when we look into the mirror? Do we look back and see that we have now changed because of this person's attitudes towards everything to include religion, just to keep the peace? Now, will we keep our current attitudes about everything because it is convenient not to revert backwards? Plus, did we make our own decisions or were we influenced somehow to change our viewpoints, thoughts, and actions by this person? Did we let them control us to the point that we are not the person we were before we met them? Should we never let ourselves change into something that we don't even recognize ever again? So many questions; I need some aspirin! So, in the words of Marty McFly in the *Back To The Future* series, "That's Heavy, Doc!"

How we respond to situations in our lifetime will build our character, in addition to our children's. If we are self-centered and everything around us must be perfect, our children will understand that they are failures before they even leave their mother's womb. I'm right, aren't I? For, if everything were perfect, we would all be happy, right? Wrong answer, Alex Trebeck! We're not on Jeopardy, and the answer is not in a mediator's hands. Think of life thus far—our faith about a higher power, and life is driven by our needs, wants, and desires. Should we wish for more in life than we currently have, or should we squander less? Plus, if we want to be faithful to a new significant other, should we pull God closer and include him in the equation? Some people may think I'm wrong. But look at life this way; if tough times are so readily available, people seem to run away from the church of which they are accustomed. If this has happened to you, you are not alone.

Think of all people, both rich and poor, who run to something or someone that makes them feel alive once again. It could be another love interest, drugs, alcohol, or something else that isn't good for them. They long for a "fix" to make everything better and/or to take away their pain. But does it really work? Probably not every time, but they keep searching. Some people never find that "fix" and they stay on a path of destruction, and they even stay single for years to avoid a relationship. Other people either throw themselves into work, volunteer jobs, or something else that takes away their recent pain or pain of long ago. Their time is so filled up, and on purpose sometimes, that they don't have moment for a significant other. Does this rescue them from their misery? Probably not. On the other hand, some people feel they must always have a special someone in their lives. They can't be alone—ever. So, they find John or Jane Doe off the street to fit the bill. This type of thinking can put them right back into the same situation they were trying to escape from in the first place. Eventually, their desire to "fill" themselves up has a way of hurting them in the end if they're not careful.

So, what makes our mind think the way we do? Is it our strength or weakness that guides us down that path of despair, destruction, or even success? Who knows? But how we approach our lives now, and the decisions we will make, will ultimately define our future. Do yourself a favor, put all your cards on the table with your next relationship. Make sure the communication is there, and you understand each other—for the most part anyway. Having an open and honest relationship from the beginning is what you must have in order to succeed this time—right? When the other person wants to talk to you—let them! I'm sure you'll be amazed by what you hear. I'm no Dr. Phil, so don't get the idea I'm always right about life. I've just lived a lifetime in the last several months, so I am sharing how it's affected me. I've felt emotions I never thought existed, but now I've grown emotionally, and it really is a good thing.

No matter what your desire is to go forward, sometimes life will pull you back a few steps when a specific date on the calendar stares you in the face. For instance, today is October 6, 2010. It was 1990 on this date that I was married to that man—Ouch! I would have been married 20 years today if I were still with him. Time flies when you're having fun, huh? That answer would be a big fat NO! When I first remembered that date this morning, I thought 19 years had passed, but it was just shy of 19 years, last year, when we split. Wow! Do I look back now and think that those were 20 years of my life wasted? Maybe some of it was, but not all. There were good times intertwined with the bad; however, the bad is what I remember the most. It's almost like how we feel about ourselves when we are growing up. If we constantly hear that we're bad, we'll remember "that" word. However, if we get that much-needed encouragement and support, we seem to have a different perspective on life and what it throws our way.

Now, with that in mind, do we need to go through tragedy to truly understand where we've been for all that time we now look back on? Or will we throw ourselves into a pity party until our feelings are all gone? Will our "wishing well" dry up with all our requests, or will it not grant our wishes at all? If we just sit around and wallow in our sorrow, it may happen—that is—nothing at all. Remember, the world turns without our permission, and it will always do so. It's how we respond when the sun rises again that counts in the end.

As I look back on "that" relationship, I think I will always have that feeling I felt for my ex, oh so long ago. I will always remember how it felt when I first met that person who was a major part of me. However, those feelings of love lost will always be there. But we will never again feel the same way about them due to their infidelity or the loss of their love they took when they left. We can always look back on those days and remember the good times.

A long time has passed since I felt those butterflies when he would look at me but, a lot of pain has caused us to be where we are now. However, these bad memories can never mesh into something good, or can it? I remember something told to me once by a woman whose husband cheated on her. Her comment was that her ex (after many years after his infidelity) told her that he still loved her. She responded with, "Well you have a funny way of showing it!" Was it the fact that he was finally ashamed of his actions of years past? Did his conscience finally slap him in the face and wake him up? Whatever his reason, his comment was not appropriate—not then, not ever.

I've recently talked with a friend of mine who has been married three times. She is now at the point in her life where things are comfortable—both financially and personally. After speaking with her about her past marriages, she is now very content with her current marriage. She told me that she believes life has a pre-determined destiny for each of us. Marriage, and life in general, involves a growth process, especially if we get married too early in life. Sometimes we only get married to please our parents, because children are involved, or for some other reason, but those decisions can come back to haunt us. If we let others direct our future with a significant other, we must live with that decision—not them, Remember that! Plus, whatever reason we equate to get married, we really do hope it is the right one.

Remember, life does not allow us to grow up just because we get married. Matrimony only seems to complicate matters when we must make adult decisions and we're not ready for them. On the other hand, if we make the decision that bringing children into the mix will "repair" whatever problem we're having, then we're really confused about life. Love and lust can make us crazy when we're young. But we sometimes want a person so badly that we will do almost anything to be with them and no one can tell us differently. So, if we end up with children in a marriage that isn't working, where do we go from here? Do we feel that we're stuck in a life that we hate, and we will never be able to do what we want now? Children should grow up in an environment where both parents want them, not just one person or neither one. An equal contribution by each parent is in order—don't you think?

Think of marriage and children this way. Our bitterness for "failure" in a marriage shouldn't be directed to our children. Even my little sister was glad she didn't have any children with her first husband. She had enough on her plate at the time of their split and if she had had any children, they all would have suffered the consequences. I truly believe that there would have been a lot of bitterness between them if there were children involved. Besides, now she is happily married and has a new daughter. I guess life has a way of preparing you now for things that happen later. It's almost like getting a vaccination; it is used to prevent us from getting a sickness—just like a divorce, huh? Too bad that vaccine couldn't be 100 percent effective!

The events that happen to us in our earlier years are the ones that make us stronger in our later life—but only if we survive the struggle. Just think how our destiny would have changed if we had a different job, a different love interest or if we had made different decisions—where we would be today? I guess things happen beyond our control sometimes, and the people who can influence us the most are our family, money, job, and of course kids.

Think of life this way—if we did have kids way back then, how would that influence us today? Would that significant other get involved and want to be around our children? Or, on the flip side, would they even want children or even grandchildren? How would they view our past lives and even their own? Would they condemn us for being married one, two, or even three times because of our infidelity or the infidelity of our significant other at the time? On the other hand, would we scrutinize them for the same thing, or for them being single for several years because they swore off marriage and relationships? Life gets a little weird sometimes, I guess, because we try to analyze our life now since we've been "without" a special person for a long time. Besides, we could be so set in our ways now that no one will fit into our world because we won't let them. We are more stubborn now and we won't accept just anyone to be our soul mate. I suppose the old proverb is to never say never. For if we think we will never meet the "right" person again, could we possibly be wrong?

Remember "Fonzie" in Happy Days? Well, he had a hard time saying the word "wrong." It seemed to always be frozen on his lips, and it would never come out like it should. Admitting we're wrong (to ourselves anyway) seems to help us grow and learn from our mistakes and others.

Lots of things can influence your actions, and your eventual decisions will take you down life's path in a certain direction. With each stumbling block, we can go down another path that we didn't see before. When we get there with that special someone, it seems the magic key is communication. For, if communication ceases, one's mind starts a conversation with itself and too many "bad" ideas seem to develop.

I guess communication should start in our home when we are very young. If our parents do not communicate with us, and really tell us how they feel deep down inside, we grow up wondering how to communicate with anyone; especially, a significant other. At least that's how I felt, and someone I recently spoke with said the same thing. His father is dying of cancer and just like mine, words they always wanted to say to us finally came out. My father told me, before he died, that he was proud of my brother and me—something I still hold dear to my heart. Why couldn't he have said that to us when we were younger or sooner than six months before he died? He, instead, had to wait until he knew his life was fading before those words touched his lips!

As for my friend, he too, is losing his father to cancer, and on his recent trip to see him, his father told him what a smart man he is and how proud he was of him. Hello? Is this generational or what? Were our parents told to keep their thoughts and feelings inside a box never be revealed until death comes knocking? I really don't get it! As for my son, each time I deliver him to his father, I always tell him that I love him. For, I never know when I will see him again—right? You know I'm right. Even my mother had those same ideals up until about a year ago, and then she started telling me she loved me. I was taken back at first, but I have realized that she knows more about life than I had originally thought.

Just think about your belief system. You learn your everyday behaviors from the time you come out of your mother's womb until the day you die. Your principles can cause you to be ridiculed, you could take things less personally, or you can let everything in life hurt you. Every event can create pain and anguish in your life, but it can happen only with your permission. Remember, that's the key—things that you may or may not have control over, end up with your final actions. I mean, the way we act when something happens, that we don't like, will ultimately be our success or our demise.

The suffering and trials we face as a child, and especially as an adult, forms our patience and perseverance. But, with our resolve, our character is eventually formed—right? For, we wouldn't truly appreciate those good times, if it wasn't for those trying times. But we must first learn that each time we are put in a position to fail, what we do to resolve it is how we ultimately learn and achieve success at the next level.

So, if we persevere in every aspect and we continually fail, have we failed in life? I don't believe so because we have learned how to move forward in adversity. Think about the generation that is growing up now. I see people who were born in the 80s and 90s and, some but not all, of them have a "want me, give me" mentality. I'm not putting them down; I'm just putting into words what I perceive by their actions. These views are ones that scream "help me," "give me," and "I deserve." I guess we all go through some of these emotions; I did when I was a teenager. Now, I look back and realize that my parents were teaching me one of life's greatest lessens when they said "No" when I wanted something that they thought was not necessary.

Failing the test of "life" can either make or even break a person; don't you think? One can decide that they can't move forward—ever—but what would this prove? This is one aspect that seems hard for some individuals when it comes to a new relationship.

Your "present" torture seems to succumb every thought and movement, which doesn't allow you to desire something better for yourself. On the other hand, we just want something new because what we currently have isn't working, but we can't achieve it. Now, I know what you're thinking. Women and men who have married more than once can still carry a torch in their heart for the "one" that got away, or for someone new who can make them whole. The "what ifs" and "I should have" in life seem to constantly be present and seem to nag us. They still seek the compassion that they truly want and deserve. Perhaps our character is only resolved by our determination or lack thereof? I know in my heart that no sane person truly wants to go through tragedy, but it seems to always be there waiting to attack us when we think life is going along fine. However, it's the understanding and lessons we get from these tests and trials in life that keeps us going—so, don't ever give up! Got it?

Now that we've gone the distance—that is—the period of our life that hurts our character as well as our soul, are we now bitter? I know that part of me still burns like fire when I think of what I went through when I got divorced. Besides, is there anyone in our life judging us for our past "mistakes"? They saw our significant other very clearly; while we stood back and either ignored their actions or put up with them. We are not as we once were. We have grown tremendously; we have felt hurt like no other person can explain, but we have survived! Wow! It's like treading water in the ocean. We hope to be rescued, but we're not sure when that will happen. However, during that time, we are struggling to survive on our own. Because we feel that we're the only person out there who is fighting this personal attack. If anything, good did come out of my divorce. I got back my faith. My every emotion was expressed to Him and some days I had no clue if I would make it to see another day. Perhaps, in the future, I can share my experience with my son when life throws him the curveballs of adulthood.

With each day and each year that passes, reflections are made on our early times. So, if we look back with remorse, are we left with bitterness or are we thankful? Did we make up our minds that those events can never be pushed aside? Plus, will we always feel hatred towards that person who put us through so many traumas? Or will we want to give them a bottle of wine and a thank you card? In my case, I chose the latter.

## 02.

## *Till Death Due Us Part Are You Kidding Me?*

As conversations come up about life, I have found that there seems to be a lack of the answers I truly need. For example, I just found out last night that a neighbor, at my last residence, died in his sleep earlier this week! He and his wife just seemed to be the perfect couple. They spent a lot of time together, constantly traveled, took care of their grandkids jointly, and seemed truly happy. They were married for over 40 years, and about four years ago relocated here to be near their children and grandchildren. Over several years, I watched both of their daughters give birth to their children, and I think he was one of the proudest grandpa's I've ever seen. I remember the days when he would walk down the sidewalk, with them in tow, as he carefully watched every step. He had the patience of a saint—with a toddler—that is. He even took my son to the tennis court several times to help him with his backhand. When they couldn't go to the court, they played in front of the house until dark. He was a former middle school teacher who went out of his way for every child in and out of the classroom in addition to the neighborhood kids.

This neighborhood, when I was with my ex, two men have died since my divorce. The stranger part is that one lived beside me and the other lived behind me. Both couples seemed to have a great relationship. Oh, I'm sure there were things that irritated each one of them about the other, but overall, their relationships worked. These four individuals made a commitment for life, but death was their ultimate key that tore both couples apart.

Again, I look back and try to relate death to divorce, but there is no comparison. I know that when a spouse cheats on you, one of the first things that come to mind is wishing they would leave the earth differently than they arrived. There is just a different range of emotions that are presented to you, both, in death and divorce, and once more, there is no handbook to find the answers to your questions. Both occasions present emptiness inside you, and confusion is your number one friend. Even if your parent passes to their reward, nothing can compare to that heart wrenching feeling of losing that person, to another, who was "once" your soul mate.

One emotion that really hits you when your partner dies is that you're mad. Yes, I said mad. Somewhere down deep, you are angry that they left you without your permission. Sounds almost comical, but it really isn't. Choosing to die isn't really an option when it is inevitable and out of our control. It's something that just happens with age, disease or whatever hits you like a lead brick. Just like divorce, death presents us with a loneliness that cannot be overcome lightly. I don't think it can ever be trumped, but that's just my opinion.

Just like divorce, years can pass, but there will always be emotions, concerns, and regret for which we can't concede. Even though we may think we can push those emotions to the side and forget them, believe me, they're still there. On the other hand, I guess when some couples say, "I Do," they really mean it. I admire those individuals who can put up with every little idiosyncrasy that the other has that drives them crazy.

One such couple that I admire are my previous neighbors that I just mentioned. I don't ever remember them saying a mean word to each other, nor did I ever hear one talking bad about the other. They would only roll their eyes, lovingly, and shake their head regarding their spouse's words, each emotion, and each habit that was present. They put up with each other's "imperfections," but still gave each other their respect.

## Attempting To Let Go

    I went up to her house this evening to see her and express my sadness for her loss. As I turned the corner, up ahead I saw his truck parked along the sidewalk. He never really parked there—it was always in the garage. But only if he was doing some yard work, did he park it outside. I think my heart sank when I knew he would never drive it again. I approached the house and then parked in the driveway. I opened my car and went around to the front door. There I found the outside light turned on as if no one would be home until later. I rang the doorbell twice, but the home was quiet. I peeked inside the side window, and the stillness was almost too much to bear. I wanted so much to give her a comforting hug, but I couldn't. It was as if they were just gone for a few hours, and they would walk back at any time. My realization, however, hit me and I knew that this was not the case.

    As I walked back to my vehicle, I had a sinking feeling about that home. For, it was 2002 that another neighbor died from cancer in that house. It brought back many sad memories once again. At that moment I knew I couldn't leave without really knowing that he was gone. I was in denial. As I started up my vehicle, I saw that a neighbor across the street was home. I stopped and rang the doorbell. I hadn't seen them in probably four months, but I was anxious to speak with them about what happened. They informed me that one day earlier this week, the paramedics, and a couple of police cars were at their house. As those words rolled off her lips, I knew I had been told the truth. I guess denial was something I made a priority since I heard about his fate last night. He was such a great man. It doesn't seem fair, does it? Why does one have to "leave" a relationship when the plan was to be together forever? But, how long is forever? On the other hand, why does it seem unmerited for a spouse to cheat, get away with it for months—even years, and then commence to make their "prior" significant other miserable for years afterward? Therein lies a myriad of questions for which we may never know the answers.

It's interesting how some relationships weather the perfect storm, but others wander as far to the left as possible. It's almost a crapshoot when a couple gets married. Whether or not it is meant to be, is the goal, in life, to be and stay married? Even after divorce, getting along with your ex (especially if you have children) is also a challenge. I know; I still struggle with that chore too. Besides, I'm still looking for that damn book, once more—you know, the "Handbook of Life." Or the one I really like (that someone should write) is, "How To Deal With Idiots Who Want to Constantly Irritate You." I sure could use one of those books right now!

Just think, as we go through this journey we call life; we seem to always be surprised at what is thrown our way. We all know there's life, death, divorce, taxes...and the list goes on. Whether death or divorce is the major thing in your life right now, both can consume you. For example, on another day, I dropped by my former neighbor's house to check on her—you know, the one I just spoke about who's husband just died—this time she was home. One of the first things she asked me was, "How did you make it by yourself?" Wow! That hit me like a lead brick, and I wasn't sure what to think. Just last year she was at my side consoling me when my ex-husband left. Her words of comfort were much needed then, just as mine were for her today. Even back then her husband had been there to hear me vent about my ex. It was then that I truly realized that having your friends and family near was something we all need when a person leaves you—whether it is death or divorce. She also told me about the neighbor behind her whose husband died almost a year ago. This neighbor still has her days and nights where survival is at its peak. But, she said, "You just get through it." No one ever said it was easy to lose that special person in your life that you have depended on for so long. But, taking one day at a time when life tosses you around is the only way. I know it sounds corny, but it's very true. I've also noticed that women seem to come back to reality faster than men. When a man loses a spouse, they are so vulnerable, and they seem to get married again very quickly after that dreaded event.

As our conversation continued, I saw her heart ache. She told me that she had talked to her four-year old granddaughter why grandpa wouldn't ever come home again. She is only four, but with tears welling up in her eyes, she seemed much more mature. Did she really understand that death had taken him? Perhaps. I guess we all deal with death differently. I remember when my granddad died; my niece was four years old too. At the funeral, she didn't have a clue what that meant. When I was seven, I remember seeing my 11-year-old cousin in a casket at the front of the church. She had died of stomach cancer—I didn't have a clue about her death either. But I still have that picture of her so vividly in the back of my mind—to this day. That video, that I made in my head, seems to always rewind to that point in my life when tragedy strikes.

We also spoke about her marriage. She told me that she had 41 wonderful years with him. They must have really respected each other in a way that I may never know. Even though she knew my marriage didn't last, she was now looking to me for answers on how to now survive. Hello? When did I become a resident expert? Therein lies the problem—I'm not an expert. I'm just getting through life like everyone else who is struggling in some form or fashion.

Anger, frustration, denial, and eventual acceptance can happen in any relationship. Whether or not it ends in death or divorce, we can be lost without that person. After a relationship ends, we also are reminded of life without them. Whether there are good or bad memories, they are always present and can flood back into our mind at any time. These memories sometimes bring emotions we can't control. We don't want to go on sometimes because we either miss that person terribly or we hate them for leaving. Right? I guess that mystery in life will always be there, but it's the way we handle it that will prepare us for "survival mode."

I guess endurance is one way to think about your current life. If your ex was there for you for everything in the beginning, but they slowly drifted away from you, at the point of divorce, life is now different. If you're not feeling well, guess what? You're on your own. There's no one in your home to comfort you and care for your illness. Perhaps your family can help—but only if they live close. Your friends are another resource, but it's not the same. Then, if you're a single parent, the "unwritten" law says a parent, especially if you're a woman, you can't get sick—your child comes first. Yikes! Each time another event happens, it seems to remind you that you're really by yourself now, and it could be permanent—but only if you allow it.

Now, think of an existence this way, where would anyone be without the challenges from their past? In addition, as we watch the sun rise each morning, do we feel regret for our past mistakes or is it a new day to succeed in another facet of your life? Do we wish we didn't have anything that challenged us?

Well, that's a no-brainer, but guess what? The things that we deal with or have dealt with in our past, and what will happen in our future, develop our coping skills. You know I'm right. But no one wants to admit it, nor do they want to experience these "things" in life that really irritate us! Life is filled with pain, anguish, and hope. But, if I stand afar and review my surroundings, can I make a better decision than a person who is in the thick of it? Well, maybe.

We all have our ideals for ourselves and for our friends and family who are in challenging positions. I guess it's the way we stand remotely from those events to the words that come out of our mouth to give comfort. My theory is that one cannot truly understand a situation unless they go through it themselves. Call me one-sided, but just think about what I just said. It's like having a baby, everyone can talk about how harsh the pain is, but no one really knows until they go through it. Even men try to compare passing kidney stones to childbirth. Hello? Men don't give birth to footballs! On the other hand, women don't know the frustrations that men go through and probably can't compare themselves to any event—so I guess we're even, huh?

I've talked about couples that split up and eventually divorce, and how great the pain is for them. What I haven't talked about is another issue I ran across recently. I met a young lady not more than 26 years old who's husband passed—he also was in his late 20s. The destruction that was in her heart was devastating. She could barely keep her composure on any question that was asked of her. At any minute I expected her to cry out in horror for her face had the look of complete loneliness and despair.

This situation can be a similar comparison to when our spouse cheats on us. On the other hand, after a couple has had a long relationship, and then one spouse dies, there is some comparison. No matter the situation, there is never a good way to say goodbye—no matter if it was either bad or good. I think the worst part of this story was that this couple had a child together under the age of three. Just think, this child would never know his father! To make the matter worse, this man was buried the day before Father's Day. Can you say OMG?

Sometimes our loved ones "check out" without our permission and leave us with the feeling of hopelessness. Divorce even touches this feeling. It's like PTSD has arrived and invaded our brain and it will never leave. Perhaps counseling could help, but it will take a long time to heal our heart. Every day we will walk with the notion that we could have helped them or our self in some way. We will ask "why" certain events happen, and every waking moment we think of them.

If we think that divorce will haunt us forever, we must first look at another area that I recently came across with an acquaintance. This situation was quite different than what divorce could ever compare with—it was suicide. A person must feel there is no way out of their situation, and taking their own life is the only answer. For those who die young, we can often wonder why their life was taken so soon. They miss out on life and what is out there to share with someone. Sometimes we can intervene with life's events; other times there is no way to change their mind. We may never know the answer as to why they left us, but we must always realize that we are to carry on their works of life. They have left us with a lesson to move forward without them. I guess when you feel that your divorce has taken every breath out of you, just remember suicide is a permanent decision—life isn't.

## 03.

## Does Marriage Equal Bliss?

At this point in this book, you're probably wondering how you've made it thus far without losing your sanity, right? Well, you may have gotten close, but believe me, it's still there—your sanity, that is! If you've had conflicts in the past, not including marriage and divorce; you know what I'm talking about. You struggle, you fight, you wrestle with your emotions, and your plans, and then you get over it—well, maybe. Wrestling with our desires can sometimes be frustrating because it can cause us to be discouraged.

We are usually presented with heavy concerns about where we want to be after a tragedy. However, it does come with important outcomes. Our knowledge and understanding of current and past events mold us more than we want to admit. Getting assistance when you or someone you know is struggling works best when you tell friends and family of those troubles, perhaps even a counselor. Remember, the most important task in your life now is to heal inside. Encouragement in your heart comes when you talk with those whom you spend time with, it's these people in your life who count the most. For, their words of encouragement are the ones that will stay in your heart forever. Keep in mind—if your ear is pierced with words of encouragement, your heart can find confidence and healing can begin. The person within those walls is ultimately who you are, and who you eventually become.

Here's something to remember. The issues of life flow through the inner parts of your bloodstream, and what really matters in life shouldn't keep you imprisoned. Your emotions are what can incarcerate you, but only if you let them. Plus, a lack of unity can contradict your ultimate plans to love once again. Completeness must begin with awareness and acceptance to form you as a whole person. With wisdom, one's eyes can be opened to see the wondrous things present that we were meant to be, feel, and ultimately become. The hurt you still feel from those people who did you wrong may stay with you forever—just remember to learn from their actions. Your experiences will then take you farther than their petty ways.

With our experience of "going before," we should obligate ourselves to speak with others of our newly found knowledge. The same hurt we have experienced can allow others to open their eyes to events currently in their life. I guess we were all given coping skills, but sometimes we need a little more help. Hugs, words of support, and just being there for a person is what everyone needs, especially if we don't realize it at the time. Only then can we see we are not alone, for when we speak of our experiences, we know that we can really survive.

Life is not fair; it's never been fair, but isn't this why God created angels for all of us? Understanding regret about a past relationship, with the same way as you first loved, is how you know you can love again. Remember, lessons learned will prepare our future coping skills when it comes to dealing with our next relationship. Only then can one make progress towards the intention of being happy once again. With that in mind, death as well as divorce affects our self-esteem because it plays a large role in our psyche. When we are alone again, new rules are in effect. So, wasn't it the plan to get married, be with that person for 40+ years, retire, and live happily ever after? Well, somewhere life got into the mix and stirred up too much crap that we can't digest all at once.

Well, think of life this way—spending your golden years with someone is the goal, right? Well, guess what? The monkey wrench that some people have in their tool chest just loosened the wrong screws between you and that significant other. Instead of using it to tighten them, it was used to strip the bolt from its placement. Now, since life isn't going the way you planned, what do you do? Feeling lost and alone is the first thing you experience, and advice from others who have gone before you are all you hear. You're not sure if their advice is warranted and if their resolution is ultimately your answer. We just need to know we will survive even though our space bubble, which has protected us up until now, is now smaller. Plus, the same situations we share with the new members of "this" group can make us stronger as a unit even though, at the time, we feel so lost and alone.

How we cope says a lot about us. You know I'm right—just think about it. When we lose that special someone in our life due to death, divorce, infidelity, or some other life-altering event, we automatically put up our guard. We get scared, we wonder about being alone for the rest of our life, if we will have the same friends ever again that we shared together, and how we will make it financially. It doesn't matter our age; for events can happen from the time we are very young up until we retire. Our health plans, our debt, our children(s) future, etc., scare us silly when our life veers off course into oblivion. No one ever prepares us for this part of our existence. I guess one way to understand, especially divorce, is to look at the national statistics. However, if we just look around at our friends, family, and co-workers, we can get a look at that big picture firsthand. I mean, last year, I had to use both of my hands to count the people I knew, including me, who were going through a divorce. There were three of us just in my immediate family! Ouch!

A crisis such as divorce is so prominent everywhere—not just in one's family. So, I recently went onto the Internet to see what statistics were out there about marriage and divorce. I was surprised to find the answers I sought. On the website www.edivorcepapers.com, here's what I found out about Colorado:

> *"1) Since 1950, more than 0.773 million divorces and more than 1.5 million marriages have been recorded in this state, 2) For a given day in Colorado, there are on an average 56 divorces and 96 marriages, and 3) The divorce rate of this state in 2003 was the least in 34 years."*

It's now 2010, and I wonder if the economy has changed these statistics. Well, my opinion is yes—for what I've seen lately, finances and infidelity, seem to be the main cause of any breakup. I even found out information from the same website why there is such a high divorce rate in Colorado. They are:

> *"1) A large percentage of the residents of this state are not natives. They have moved to this state from other states and consequently have no or little support structures, 2) Most*

*of the population in this state is young and these people are recreationally oriented and do not believe in long-term relations, 3) This state has one of the highest cohabitation rates and generally cohabitating relations result in failed marriages, and 4) A major section of the population in this state is un-churched. It has been proved by research that those marriages that have a specific faith foundation have a better rate of survival."*

Some of these facts held true in my relationship with my ex. We had both moved from different states, but he had been here for several years before we met. I was here only one year before I met him. Also, he had no desire to attend church for he had "lost" his religion somewhere down that path of life. As for me, mine was misplaced for a while, but now it's back.

Now that we know about divorce statistics, don't we wonder why people remarry? Are we that lonely that we must find Ms. or Mr. Right? Do we long for another person who will take the place of that person we desired to be with at one time in our lives? I really think we do want someone to hold our hand, tell us we're special, and will ultimately love us till "death due us part."

So, now that you've been through that "divorce thing," just think back on how it affected your life. For females after they've gone through a divorce their standard of living drops 45 percent—this was a survey done in 2000 by the National Center for

Health Statistics. Whoa! Who was the idiot that said that women should suffer more than men or vice versa? Do men get off scott free when they just walk away from a relationship? Or do women do the same thing and feel nothing? Just think "fatherless homes" are linked to 63 percent of youth suicides, 90 percent of homeless/runaway children, 85 percent of children with behavior problems, 71 percent of high school dropouts, 85 percent of youths in prison, and 50 percent plus of teen mothers according to the <u>National Center of Health Statistics</u>.

In the <u>Journal of Marital and Family Therapy</u>, it is reported that, especially for men, marital problems are associated with decreased work productivity. Say what? Does their ego get in the way of them loving their significant other for now their self-worth is gone and they need greener pastures? Perhaps. I know that when I was going through my divorce, the level of concentration that I needed to survive was non-existent. The roller coaster that I was on continued to throw me around so much that my productivity at work was very much affected. I really feel that if I had more support from my manager at work, while I was going through this time, my concentration wouldn't have left me so easily. However, I was told that I needed to put that part of me aside and concentrate on work (as if nothing was going on in my life). Hello? Was there no brain function left in this manager to feel compassion? I know that my brain was having a hard time putting itself around too much information, because my entire way of living had changed. But I guess it's quite easy for someone to not put themselves in another one's shoes, especially if they have never been there themselves. I was extremely saddened by her attitude towards me because it was unwarranted and not expected. I hope that someday the chalice on her heart will heal and her empathy will return.

Maybe it's the way society has changed since the 50s. Cohabitation is something that is readily accepted now and marriage has been taken off its highest pedestal. Marriage is not as much of a priority as it once was, and statistics don't lie. A random phone survey by *Stanley and Markman (Journal of Marriage and the Family)* stated that many more couples live together now prior to marriage than in the past. A recent estimate of people has revealed that 60 percent plus—are together without a marriage bond. In addition, these couples are less likely to stay together because they view marriage and divorce in a very conservative way.

As years pass in a relationship, money is the one thing that people say they argue about most in a marriage, followed by children (*Stanley and Markman, nationwide phone survey*). But there is reason to believe that what couples argue about is not as important as how they argue (*Markman, Stanley, and Blumberg, 1994*). Whatever the reason, when arguments get out of hand, sometimes there is no way to "fix" the situation, divorce can rear its ugly head quite quickly, and says, "Hello, never thought you'd see me, huh?

With everything in life that we must deal with after a divorce, and the longer I'm single, the more I hear about marriages that are not working. Don't get me wrong; maybe someday I will do it again—you know, say "I Do." However, right now when I hear the word, "marriage," I feel shivers down my back, and I think the hairs on the nap of my neck stand up at attention. Wow! What happened? I mean, if a person gets married, gets divorced, and has bad feelings about the whole process, should they write off marriage ever again? Or does it take years to realize that marriage isn't so bad, but only if both parties work at it? The trick is to find the right person the first time; I guess. Yeah, right! Well, that's a no-brainer, huh? Isn't there an "app" for that for my life? Well, I'm sure if someone can figure out that question, someone will invent one. Crazy, huh?

Life's little handbook never had a chapter like this! Maybe I'm just picker now—perhaps I don't want to go through that "BS" again? However, I guess that "part" of my life is always going to be very close and always nagging at me. Just think, when you do make that plunge again by putting yourself out there, what will you think? Remember this—each day, each month, and each year that goes by, in a new relationship, it seems to reveal a little more about you and your new significant other. Each new conversation and action about past or forthcoming events show them or us a little more about each one's personality and values. What will each of us think about this new information? Will it be the one thing that makes or breaks our new relationship? Will it be information about a child, or an abortion they had long ago that the other person never knew about? Will it be anything about their childhood, family life, or upbringing that still haunts them? Plus, does it involve emotional abuse we suffered as a child, and will it have any bearing on us now? Moreover, does this information really matter?

Should we judge a person on what happened in times past, or how they act today? Just think dating again after a divorce seems to bring new challenges, and new rules. Ok, whoever thought up this crap? Between family situations and years between being single and wanting to date, life becomes another complicated story—once again. I guess there are a lot more things to think about this time around, and a lot more at stake. It just needs to be weighed and measured—just like making a recipe from scratch. Once the ingredients are mixed, something sweet can be the ultimate outcome. If we only evaluate each item that needs to be added to the mix, not the ultimate outcome, we may see the clouds' part. Unfortunately, there are times where we cannot see how this addition to our lives can make us feel better and thrive.

Think of life this way. Our root system causes us to grow, or it will cause us to become root bound. If we compare an aspen tree's roots to our own, there are several differences. A clump of aspen trees has the same root system, so they are bound as a unit. Unlike trees, our root system can always be changed or torn apart; we just need to put forth the effort to make it thrive. With this in mind, we can get discouraged and have a lack of unity in our lives. So, what holds our mind and our body together? Are we motivated by a new love affair after we failed in our past relationships? Well, think of your situation this way. Our knowledge and understanding about what we want is a major factor in how we handle life. Just think, the more we handle the truth in our lives; the more we will know the meaning and the presence of a lie. I guess we should always look out for that wolf with persuasive words dressed in sheep's clothing. This person could ultimately become the leader in a new relationship who gains more from it than you do. So, we must be watchful in all things we do, or eventually it will become our downfall.

So, if we really know a person—or think we do—is it really fact in our eyes? If we break someone's spirit by riding him or her too hard, are we destroying that relationship forever? Plus, as we look back, do we now realize that perhaps we provoked our significant other by finding fault in them and not the good? Is it only now that we can look at our earlier experiences, and realize that we could have prevented our demise?

Or did they do the same to us, which made us act the way we did? So, now we have two people hurting deeply, with no finality in sight. Well, guess what, we can't go back in time to fix that, right?

So, did we even love each other from the beginning or was it just lust? Are two people ever meant to be together and how do we even know that answer? I guess it's how we value something in our lives, from the beginning, that will show us the answer. I just wish I could have seen, without those blinders on, from the day I first met him. A lot of time has passed now, and I have realized much about my former marriage. The most valuable lesson I leaned was that he didn't value women. He only wanted me for sex, cleaning the house, caring for our son, and watching his dog. I was a fool, and I didn't even know it for years. I still don't know how my self-worth and independence escaped me for all this time.

Remember this, when we place a value on something, such as a relationship, we become meticulous about its care. We hold it dear to our hearts, and special concern should be taken not to destroy it. If we get to a point when we care less than what we should, we allow "our garden" to go into oblivion. We don't tend to it; and, we don't nurture it. We let it die because it doesn't hold a special place in our lives anymore. Right?

It's just like a marriage and every other relationship in our existence that is lacking in love.

Showing you don't care about someone can be very hurtful—for, they don't matter any more. The respect that was once alive and flourishing is now gone. We also, as partners, sometimes don't understand what we did wrong to make it go awry. It's only after careful examination that we see the ultimate path that was taken—by both people. The ultimate goal is to make sure that we don't repeat our actions if we meet a new person to replace the one, we just lost.

I don't know about you, but it's exhausting to find a new person to fulfill your happiness. Should we even try? That's what each person must decide for him or herself. Plus, if we think that we have found that "one" once again we may, after some time has passed, realize that they don't fit the bill or even fulfil the romance we required. So, shouldn't we be with that person who completes us? Of course!

Now, are we at the point that we look back and realize that we've "failed" once again? Really? Do we have to go there once more? Has our past not taught us what we really need in a relationship, or did we not learn what love really should be from the time we were young? I guess it's like getting married more than once and each time it ends in divorce. Have we finally realized that we are to the point where we "feel" we must have a significant other in our lives to feel whole? I've known both men and women who think this way, and it seems so depressing to me.

Don't we have to be 100 percent okay with ourselves before we can invite someone to join our circle? Sounds like a plan to me! Do we feel so disconnected that we can't even function by ourselves? If we can't select thoughts on how we should live our lives, where do we go from here? Do we need God to send us a flashing stop sign when he knows we're going to make a major mistake in the next relationship? Geez, I just wish I had more answers to life's stinking questions!

Let's look at ourselves closely. If our relationship fails, do we beat ourselves up every chance we get because we miss what we had? Do we obsess over not being with them, for now they are gone—perhaps forever? We can feel like a failure or even grieve until the devotion in that relationship is gone. But we have to remember that sometimes we can't control ourselves when we separate from a "lost" connection. We must first forgive ourselves before we can forgive the circumstance—remember, we are as important as anyone else!

Coming together as a couple can mean leaving a part of you behind. We may not believe it, but we really do. In almost every case, we give up an element of what we once were. We now compromise and every decision is or should be made together. It's only when the admiration and kindness for that special person dwindles that we feel lost and alone once more. We sometimes forgave them when they strayed and patched up what was left, but other times we feel regret and perhaps blame ourselves for their actions. In other times, we blamed them for the hurt and pain we now feel and cannot shake. Then there were the times we felt we put up with "their" actions, and now we can't revisit those moments at any cost. Our past experiences with them got us to the point where we were tired of putting up with their lack of respect for ourselves. I've been there; believe me. Everyone around me saw it, but I chose to look the other way for a very long time. Should I be blamed for staying so long? I guess that is the ultimate question. However, the people who saw "him" as he really was and still is, have stood by me and now tell me how much better off I am without him. I can do better in the next relationship; I must look harder this time. The warning signs are always there in a relationship; it's only if a person wants to open their eyes and see this person who can make or break their spirit.

There is one thing that have I noticed about marriages that have gone down the path of divorce. At least one person seems to grow wings and take flight, while leaving the other one in the dust. It may not be true for everyone, but I've seen it in my life and in others who are so much happier after their initial split.

One friend of mine who has been married and divorced twice has lost almost 50 pounds! As she looked back, she admitted to me that she doesn't have good judgment when it comes to picking men. To me, it sounds like she's getting her life in check now and I told her a man is on his way to fulfill her! She let me know that the man upstairs needs to be involved in that decision! But, think about it, she is taking charge and planning her life. She's not letting anyone on this earth tell her what she can or cannot do when it comes to taking care of herself. Strong women surround me, and I'm proud of each one of them! Just remember we can be broken, but not taken out—at least not entirely.

## 04.

### *If* I Can Accomplish It, It Isn't A Problem Right?

Ok, now you're alone again. Every decision you make is your own. Every bill that comes in the mail belongs to you, and every move you make may or may not come back to haunt you. You feel lonely when you're by yourself because the silence is deafening. You long for someone to sleep beside you in that king-size bed that is now to big— for just you, and you alone. If you're by yourself due to his or her infidelity, you wonder what your ex is now doing with "their" new someone. If you're alone because your significant other died, you wonder what you could have done to save their life. We feel sad, guilty, confused, mad, belittled—you name it, it exists in your soul.

In either instance, we all want to be happy once again. Does that mean we get married once more just because we don't want to be alone? Well...maybe. Then, to make matters worse, do we choose just anyone who will fill out that prescription for which loneliness gave us, because the doctor ordered it? Our heart must choose our fate and that new special someone. Just think, in America, alone, almost 75 percent of people who get divorced remarry within four years after their divorce. Another interesting statistic shows that around 33 percent of divorcees remarry within one year after their divorce. The final statistic I found was that in 50 percent of marriages, in the United States, one of the spouses is on their second, third, fourth, or whatever marriage. Holly Cow! Are we that lonely?

I guess each revolution of the earth doesn't do much for relationships, huh? As for men, they seem to have overseen relationships and the workforce for hundreds of years. Then, women got their chance for equality and to enter the workforce as far back as WWII. In the 60s, women burned their bras and became feminists; in the 70s and 80s, women still fought for equality—both in the military and in the civilian world. Today, women are still fighting the fight to get the same respect as men in the workforce, as well as in relationships.

Think of associations, in this way—some relationships are not created equal, while others are shared 50/50. Even cohabitation was an alternative in the 80s and 90s. Were relationships better off when they weren't made legal by a ceremony and a marriage certificate? Plus, do we have those same feelings for our significant other when we don't have a circle or diamonds and gold around our finger? These questions are relevant for both men and women. Personally, they confuse the hell out of me!

Even in different countries, divorce seems to have a stigma. In some Asian nations, individuals who divorce and then remarry are shamed and dishonored. In Nigeria, if death or divorce occurs, the person affected seems to remarry rather quickly. In the Dominican Republic, the remarriage rate in the 1990s dropped due to financial reasons. One statistic showed this was due to a worsening job market, and when men are unemployed. Needless-to-say, those women opted to be a single parent instead of marrying again. Yikes!

Statistics such as these reveal something about society. Those things that have happened in our past sometimes affect what lies ahead. Whom we encounter, in our future, is a challenge if we want to find the right person again. For, now we have learned what we want out of life after a relationship has ended—or have we? This time, we either want better for ourselves because we never had it in our previous marriage, or we just want to replace those qualities we had in that soul mate who just died. On the other hand, if we are only familiar with a relationship that constantly creates chaos, and we are comfortable with that relationship, should we ultimately seek another relationship that is similar? Scary thought, huh?

In a way, we all must understand statistics about marrying again. There was a study done in 1995 that stated the following:

All races of women who were 15 to 44 years of age found the following:

| Year After Divorce | Percentage of Remarriage |
|---|---|
| 1 | 15% |
| 3 | 39% |
| 5 | 54% |
| 10 | 75% |

Another category reviewed women less than 25 years of age:

| Year After Divorce | Percentage of Remarriage |
|---|---|
| 1 | 17% |
| 3 | 41% |
| 5 | 57% |
| 10 | 81% |

Women who were more than 25 years of age had these startling statistics:

| Year After Divorce | Percentage of Remarriage |
|---|---|
| 1 | 14% |
| 3 | 37% |
| 5 | 51% |
| 10 | 68% |

I guess statistics such as these can make us wonder what makes our brain tick. Especially, since divorce or death of a spouse brings with it a new mindset. Another way to look at divorce is to understand its different aspects. Being a civilian is one scenario, but being in the military has a whole new set of rules. The long absences from one another, the pressures of being in a combat zone, and dealing with a chain of command with uncontrolled pressure can take a toll on a person and on their spouse. Besides, these men and women are defending our country. But do they have more pressure to perform as a "perfect family unit"—with the military and in their personal lives? Perhaps.

Being on call for seven days a week is the norm in the military. They don't quit after an 8am - 5pm day at the office. Our military is on call constantly, and the pressures can get to them rather quickly. I guess it's like getting migraine headaches, no one can tell you how intense the pressure can be unless you experience one. So, are statistics the only thing that really tells us the scorecard of life on another scale? The answer to that question is different for everyone, but the reality always hurts those who have been betrayed.

Think of divorce this way; during fiscal years 2006 to 2007, the Department of Defense's (DOD) statistics portrayed a 3.3 percent rate in divorce, while in 2008 it rose to 3.4 percent. So, the trend has steadily increased in just a few years. Now, to understand how divorce is viewed in the military, the chart below shows divorce statistics in the armed forces.

| Services | Overall Divorce Rate | Officer Divorce Rate | Enlisted Divorce Rate |
|---|---|---|---|
| Army | 3.5 | 2.3 | 3.9 |
| Air Force | 3.5 | 1.6 | 4.1 |
| Navy | 3.0 | 1.5 | 4.1 |
| Marine Corps | 3.5 | 1.6 | 3.5 |

Military Divorce Statistics (male/female)

| Services | Male Divorce Rate | | | Female Divorce Rate | | |
|---|---|---|---|---|---|---|
| | 2006 | 2007 | 2008 | 2006 | 2007 | 2008 |
| Army | 2.5 | 2.6 | 3.0 | 7.9 | 8.1 | 8.5 |
| Air Force | 2.6 | 2.9 | 2.9 | 6.2 | 6.5 | 6.5 |
| Navy | 2.9 | 2.8 | 2.5 | 6.9 | 6.5 | 6.3 |
| Marine Corps | 2.9 | 3.0 | 3.2 | 7.1 | 8.1 | 9.1 |

In 2004, divorce in the military increased, but if you compare the differences between officers' verses enlisted, the numbers were dramatic—3,325 Army officers, vice 7,152 enlisted members. However, in 2005, military personnel were offered counseling programs related to divorce, and the number of divorces plummeted by 61 percent. By 2005, the numbers looked as such: 1,292 Army Officers, and 7,075 enlisted members got divorced. The number of officers getting divorced went down from 6 percent in 2004 to 2.3 percent in 2005.

Some of these statistics can possibly be accounted for by the programs put into place such as weekend retreats for military couples and support groups for spouses of deployed personnel. The Army also put into place a program to help single soldiers to make in-depth decisions in selecting their mate—Premarital Interpersonal Choices and Knowledge (P.I.C.K), a Strong Bonds Marriage Education Program (for couples in the Reserve and National Guard), and several others. These programs were designed to make individuals aware of how family relationships can be strengthened or pulled apart by a soldier's absence and their return from a deployment. They were developed to help a soldier adjust with unavoidable changes due to stress that always seems to be present.

Another fact that seems to be a big difference between enlisted and officers is the fact that enlisted men and women, on average, are younger. As for women in the military, they are two times more likely to file for divorce. Research has also proved that current programs offered don't support their family.

So, what do we consider when we think about infidelity as a divorce statistic? Basically, the definition is that one person is not loyal to the other outside that marriage bond, and adultery is one example of infidelity. Think about it. In the United States alone, 17 percent of divorces are caused by infidelity. Hello? What happened to those vows we once thought would be the pathway to our eternity?

The hurt, the pain, and the next decisions we make can come from that partner who cheated on us who has now outlined our future without our permission! Ouch!! Now that we have decided that infidelity is wrong, do we all think it should be a crime? A survey I found said that:

- *61 percent are of the opinion that it should not be,*
- *35 percent thought it should be, and*
- *4 percent did not have any opinion*

Ok, now we have viewed marriage and divorce and the reasons for both. Have we become such an accepting society that we think it is the norm to expect men and women to cheat on their spouse? Then, if we accept this monstrosity, are we just as forgiving as the next person who has cheated, or have we just ignored immorality? One study, in 1997, suggested that 14 percent of women and 22 percent of men admitted sexual relations with another individual—other than their married partner. Plus, 54 percent of married men and 70 percent of married woman had no idea these antics were happening. Have we turned a blind eye, or do we really trust our partner that much? Whatever the answer, our faith in our significant other has diminished and we either don't care, or we don't think it will ever happen to us. Whether or not it happens, early in our life or later in life, it can still happen. This study goes on to say that when a couple is married, 14 percent of married woman and 22 percent of married men had an affair at least once.

Ok, where did that book on infidelity go? Is it the thrill of secrecy or an explosion of emotions built up over time that needs to be expressed to another? However, or whatever the reason, we as humans have a desire to feel good. If we meet someone at work or just flirt on a consistent basis, some people will always have those thoughts that veer from our marriage vows. So, think about it, would you have an affair if you knew you would never get caught? On the other hand, if an affair has been revealed, which usually lasts at least two years, a very small percentage of marriages do survive.

Does our attitude about infidelity start before we get married the first time? Perhaps a second, third, or fourth marriage will be different? Plus, are we willing to acknowledge to our next partner that we have committed this sin against the last person we once were committed to? Then, we must wonder what the trust factor will be in this new relationship. Will we give ourselves an excuse why we did what we did to our last relationship? Will they accept it and if they do understand, is it because they did the same in their last relationship? On the extreme side of this topic, the Internet has allowed us to go beyond just affairs with words to a person we have not met. The access to pornography and various sins allowed on certain Internet sites has let us commit these actions secretly.

A poll by www.MarriageAdvice.com in 1996, revealed optimistic statistics on what keeps marriages together. This poll had responses from 700 people who said the following:

- *30% stayed together due to love*
- *30% stayed together because of children, and*
- *20% stayed together out of commitment.*
- *Trailing behind in the poll was 9% who stayed together out of fear,*
- *8% due to finances and*
- *4% due to tradition.*

So, if we are staying together because of love or for our children, are we really committed to either one? On the other hand, if we dissolve our marriage because we don't love that person anymore, are we just grasping for ideas to leave? Either way, we need a lot of energy to accomplish our goal in life—being with that special someone. Marriage takes work. It's never easy due to the time and energy that is involved, but it's a necessary evil for success to be the ultimate outcome.

The Senior Editor of www.MarriageAdvice.com, Beth Young, advises several ways to keep your marriage strong and to stay in love. The first thing she advises is to communicate with your spouse daily on your thoughts and feelings and what is happening. One effort is to stay connected to your spouse; show them your support during difficult times and happiness during the good times. Secondly, and this sounds trivial, be sure to schedule a weekly date night. It doesn't have to be anything expensive—just time well spent together. Thirdly, make sure your spouse knows you are thinking of them—it could be a note, a thoughtful gift, a quick phone call, etc. Sometimes it's the simple things that mean the most—it's just making sure you take time to do it. Your spouse will feel special and know that you are there for them.

Doesn't being obligated to your children mean you have to stay married—Hmmm? I guess it's easier said than done, but I've known people who have stayed married even though they're totally miserable. But who are we to judge them for their actions? Like I've said before, a person must be at a "done" point in their lives before they will change their lifestyle. They must know, in their heart, that nothing will ever get better unless they take it upon themselves to go in a different direction. However, do they know something that the rest of us don't? Besides, sometimes life sends us in a direction that we never would have chosen for ourselves, so it's not all bad.

The negative impact on children, from their parent's divorce, affects not just you, but many others around you. The decision that is made to divorce needs to be weighed for every kind of impact. But are we punishing ourselves if we don't leave that relationship? Or are we just trying to protect our children to have a "family unit" that looks complete? Plus, will our decision to leave or to stay ruin the relationship our children have with us—their parents? Many factors need to be considered when divorce is in the mix. A couple needs to weigh all the factors in a breakup, but for the most part this is not done. Opportunities and actions are contemplated and made by one or both in a relationship and they don't realize how the hurt and pain can affect so many around them. My friend, Leslie, evaluated her entire situation before coming to a decision to leave her husband earlier this year. She wanted that "family unit," but she finally realized that there was no way it would ever exist. I guess she finally concluded that it was best for her and her children to split from her ex to escape a situation that would never get better.

Just think, "back in the day," our parents stayed married—for the most part—based upon commitment. Was this a reflection of their values back then, or did they just suck it up and deal with all the crap that can happen in their relationship? Did they just stick it out when they just wanted to quit? Today's society seems to have changed and changed dramatically from our parent's day. I guess it's too easy to change our minds about our "soul mate," toss them to the side, and then trade in your "40" something model for two "20s"—scary huh?

Now, here's an update I know you've waited for, for a long time. Remember my co-worker, Mary? Well, today, November 5, 2010, she is finally free. I texted her today and told her it was time for her to finally join me and the others, who have gone before her, into the Cougar Club. When she called today, she had so many feelings inside that it flowed out of her soul. She was happy, confused, crying, and wondering what her future held. She even stood up for herself and told the judge that she didn't want any alimony from her ex. Holy Cow! Where did she find her strength? Wherever her strength was hidden for all those years, it sure came out today. I'm so glad she's past this point in her life. For now, I truly believe that she can accomplish anything. This was a big step for her, and since her separation from her ex over a year ago, and with every incident that happened at this time, her mental anguish took its toll. Now that she has her "true" freedom, I know she will make it.

The choices we make today can reflect on our past events. The success and happiness we once had in a marriage that went array is something we will always long for, but we know we can never have it ever again with that person. The one thing we need to realize is that we are on our own when it comes to our happiness. We should never rely on a significant other to make us totally complete, for we can surely be disappointed.

Remember that we allow our emotions to control us, but only if we give them permission. Plus, how we handle another person's reaction to anything is our decision alone. If we allow a person to treat us poorly, it's our choice and no one else's. We can let it get to us, or we can realize what a worthless idiot they are, tell them where to go, and then get over the sarcasium rather quickly. Right? Well, choosing to be a victim in a relationship is a decision that can come from a marriage without the love it sorely needs. So, can we justify our anger and remorse because of that situation? Possibly. But, if we don't fix the wrong in our situation, it will continue, and our souls will become dented with hopelessness.

More marriage and divorce statistics from Marty Friedman, author of *"Straight Talk for Men About Marriage—What Men Need To Know About Marriage and Woman Need To Know About Men,"* and founder of www.meninmarriage.com states that there are fewer people married now. The percentage of the married population is 59 percent. In 1990, that number was 62 percent. It was even higher in 1970 at 72 percent. On the other hand, the population who has never been married is 24 percent.

Now, remember the 50s? One such show called *Father Knows Best* portrayed a family in which only the husband had a job outside the home and the wife stayed at home and cared for the children. Today this scenario is increasingly rare. In a family unit such as this, the percentage is only 22.4 percent. On the other hand, married couples where only the wife is employed is 6.8 percent. However, in marriages where both partners are employed, the percentage rises significantly to 53.5 percent.

Things have changed over the years and the economy, among other factors, has changed the dynamics of a relationship. A union seems to start out with excitement and hope for the future, but at what point of a relationship does it get harder? Statistics say that the seventh year of marriage is the hardest. The **U.S. Census Bureau** states that the median duration of first marriages that end in divorce vary slightly from male to female. For males it is 7.8 years; for females it is 7.9 years. For second marriages ending in divorce, males have a rate of 7.3 years, and for females, it is 6.8 years. Median duration of second marriages that end in divorce: Males 7.3 years, Females: 6.8 years. The **National Center for Health Statistics** states that the divorce rate increased almost 40 percent from 1970 to 1975—that was the 20th century; it's now the 21st century—what the heck happened? From 1980 to 1990 the divorce rate rose almost 10 percent. In 2000, the percent of males divorcing was 8.3 percent as compared to females—10.2 percent.

Although the divorce rate seems to be out of control, most adults *really* want to be married. Think about it. When your friend breaks up from a relationship—whether it is a dating or marriage situation, the only thing, sometimes, that makes them feel better is to have another significant other in their lives. They want that compassion and feeling of being wanted. This sense of self worth is more valuable than gold sometimes. Right? Well, the statistics don't lie. By the time people reach their 55th birthday, 95 percent of males and females have been married.

Even though we sometimes fail at marriage, we still seem to need that sense of security in our lives. Besides, isn't it the old saying that half of all marriages fail anyway? Well, in 1997, the statistics proved this to be true. So, after we're done with marriage "Number One", guess what? There is a 60 - 70 percent chance of remarriages ending in divorce. Even couples that live together don't have the ultimate romance. For, if they get married, they have a 70 percent chance of divorcing. Also, from the time couples are married for five years, they have an 82 percent chance of divorcing versus couples that have been married for 50 years—they only have a 5 percent chance of divorcing.

There's a lot of guidance out there; we just have to have a desire to find it. For, we must be watchful in all the things that are present in our lives. Especially, the people who are false—you know, those people you can't believe any word that comes from their mouth? On that note, we must change ourselves on the inside to change our outward actions. Remember, we must willingly come to a relationship or allow love to come into our lives; we can't be forced, because it won't work otherwise. Besides, if we allow God to be the guidance, he can be our stretcher, not our crutch. So, by establishing our root system with that higher power, we can get through any crisis.

## 05.

## *Embracing the Storm?*

I guess one of the things that we must look at in life is what do we truly need when our experience with marriage doesn't work? What are we willing to never again accept, and what concerns are and are not negotiable next time? There's always an opportunity for us to succeed—whether we realize it. This time is our opportunity to excel, so we must stand up for what we know won't work the next time. Now, remember to grow in your faith by remembering those words in the Bible that will give you confidence. If you do, you'll become more thankful—and not just in your daily life.

I guess it's interesting how we embrace the storm of divorce. The first year after you're "free" brings with it many challenges, and the sorrow that we feel which never really goes away. Just think, years later it can sneak back and bite you, where you think your heart once was once located. But don't we try to constantly avoid conflict once that decree is final? I know I have and sometimes I still feel very alone and scared. Would another relationship "fix" me? Or do I need to always be strong to show my son that I can make it in the mist of this storm? I know I must first learn patience with everything I now do and say. For, a storm exposes one's weaknesses, but we must rely on God's strength to carry us through. Sometimes our faith is the only thing we have left. Remember, that stretcher isn't far away when we need it because those hands are ready to catch us when we are at our weakest.

So, why are we worried when He isn't? Sounds like a rhetorical question, huh? But being faithful, when the storm hits you hard, can take a toll on you even though your friends and family are there to be by your side. When you think everyone has deserted you, there are people around us to give their support. For instance, I had cousins that I hadn't talked to in years, call me and tell me what an ass he was when I was in the mist of my divorce. Yes, I was surprised and shocked because they were there for me, and I never knew it! They reiterated my suffering, and their words of support were what I needed to see though another day.

Our faith can be reaffirmed during that storm, and the weakness we feel can be helped by that devotion. I guess we never really know how strong we can become until we are put through the test of life. Remember, our strength can lead to our victory and to our success. It's easier said than done, but with each step, it is possible. Just make peace with your world when there is turmoil; things will work out for the good. Just think of tragedy like this. At the scene of a forest fire there are ashes all around, but the beauty is located beneath the rubble just waiting to show itself. The smoldering ruins eventually produce green grass and new growth. Flowers and seedlings will become evident within months even though everything above ground is charred. Sounds incredible, but at the bottom of each trial, the only way to go is up. So, with each weapon that is thrown at you, remember God provides you with a shield to protect yourself.

Now that you're passed that point of constant sorrow, tears, and helplessness, remember to make the space in your life where turmoil once was positioned. Now there is room in your life to make plans and get involved in the things you once yearned for, because now the space is available. Before, your thoughts and feelings consumed you and there was no freedom for anything else. Now the concentration you had for your marriage can be focused on healing yourself.

I just know that the first year after divorce doesn't heal everything. Those same feelings of confusion are still there, and I don't think they ever go away—even with time. Your bitterness and attitude can still haunt you even though finding the end of the storm is just out of your reach. Just remember, every storm you now face has a purpose. Learning and growing from each event will continue your reasons to grow in life.

I guess when we get to a specific point in our lives—after divorce, that is—we can let everything else around us complicate our lives just as much. Things that happen to our kids, our friends, and our parents weigh just as heavily as our divorce once did. When there is no control on the happenings around us, we feel helpless and powerless to do anything. Once more, we experience the victory of defeat. We could feel we have been cheated out of what life could have given us to make us happy. We can throw all the money we want into these problems, but most of the time it doesn't fix them. We could throw up our hands and walk away, but what does this prove? If we chased after philosophy or traditional ways, would we be better off? If we adapted to tradition, it could also cause problems. For, sometimes we don't know why we do what we do since we've always done it "that" way.

The hurt and pain that still linger from a divorce isn't very far away from our hearts. Years can pass and life's events can be a very hurtful reminder of that lost love. Even events that our children and family put us through can also be painful. Especially when we don't have a "quick fix" answer. We want them to succeed in everything they do, and when we don't know where to turn, our heart aches for them. It's a gentle reminder from when our ex hurt us in that past time, causing our hearts to break. Some days I don't have any answers, but I keep searching. One day I will find those answers I so desperately need today. God help me in my time of need!

As the days and months go by, I am realizing that each crisis I am presented with seems to make my heart sink. That gut-wrenching feeling I had when I first found out that my ex was cheating seems to come back rather quickly with each new predicament. Each medical crisis that my friends or I must deal with hurts just as much as before I found out my future fate. Maybe it's the fact that I feel I have no control over the outcome? Perhaps it's the fact that I don't have a book of answers or a lucky charm to prevent the next crisis? I guess we all struggle for the answers we so desperately need and want. It's only after going through a difficult time that we realize that life never gets any easier, for a new challenge is always waiting around the corner to greet us.

With each event in our life, we seem to get a new set of skills to help us identify and cope with the next crisis. But do we ever get to the point of wanting to let life really get us down that we don't want to be here anymore? Some people may think so, but what

Attempting To Let Go

do they prove to themselves and others around them if they "check out" of life? They leave behind tragedy for others to deal with—what a "chicken-shit" way of coping—by taking the easy way out! I'm right and you know it.

I've known people who have taken their lives just because they thought they had no other choice. I've also known of people who will say they will "check out" but don't because they just want the attention of others. Their cry for help is there; we just must identify it and save them from themselves, even though our dislike for them can be so ever present.

Is it constant attention we need to feel important or is it just our main reason to exist? Sometimes we must find our motivation to get up, get dressed, and find a rationale to continue living. Some days are harder than others, but there is a purpose for us to be here on earth—we just need to find it. I know that lately I'm having more challenges than normal. It seems like it was just a week ago my life was in turmoil, and then a day later it all ceased. Now, it has returned with full force to make me find more answers to life's little irritating questions.

One of the issues I am facing is that my ex and I must work closely together once more. It feels strange that we are functioning as a single unit—almost like we are forced to take care of things, but now it's different. We are talking like we did in the days when we worked together. The words between us are calming and well thought out. We are planning things for our son to prepare him for his future. The challenges are still there between us, but now something is different. We are not looking at his and my faults, our past dealings, and insensitive words that were said to each other that hurt so badly. The old saying, "...and this too shall pass," really has hit home once again. I think the spaceship is coming in for a landing, maybe not.

I'm not sure what to think anymore. But one thing that I do know is that I am trying to come to the realization that I'm ok with myself. On the other hand, I sometimes feel that I am slowly losing my authority because I am in a little red wagon flying down a hill out of control. I guess at some point each one of us must guard themselves against the burden of life. When the lack of commitment in relationships also becomes lacking in other areas of life, challenges can be so hurtful. Wanting that much needed hug when you hurt inside is something we can ponder over way too much. Especially, when we can't find someone to give it to us.

Commitment to our religion can also challenge us when life seems so complicated. There is a bigger picture of what needs to happen to keep us whole and God must be present so we can keep our sanity. He provides us with love, power, and a sound mind. So, when the heaviness in our heart is present, just remember to look toward the heavens. This heaviness can be a very significant turning point because new places, events and people can cause us to become overwhelmed and/or uncomfortable. Remember, when your eyes are shut, darkness is all around. But where there is light, darkness cannot dwell—it shall flee, right? Well then—open your eyes!

The same goes for relationships. If you open yourself up once again, there is a chance that good can come from it—you just need to trust in yourself. However, we must first stand back and evaluate what we're getting into, once again. Does it feel right? Is there anything that bothers us when we think about the whole picture? It doesn't matter if we're trying to get back into a relationship after we've lost our significant other due to death or divorce. Remember, the storm is always there—we just to remember that we need an umbrella, so we won't get soaked! The storm can rage all around us; the dark clouds can be angry with lightning, and rain can pour down all around us. But it's our shelter that protects us, it just needs to be defined.

I guess when we are at our lowest point; we must once again look to the man above and ask for guidance. Our tears and our frustration should be the first indicator that there is something wrong in our lives. When we don't have the answers to life's questions, He does. I know. I've leaned very heavily towards asking for his assistance for the past year and a half. The more crises that have happened, the more I need answers for the direction I need to precede towards. Some issues take longer to resolve, but we need to put our patience into play and realize that we can't have a quick fix every time.

Sometimes it seems we are grasping for that last straw when it comes to losing that one, we love. It could involve our significant other, a friend, or more importantly a parent. It's still the case—we are never prepared on what to do or how to finalize the situation. We have pains in our heart, our appetite lessens, and we want to crawl into a hole and escape. But we can't. We are put into a position where we cannot get away and we are forced to deal with it to the end. We still hurt—sometimes deeply. We wonder what keeps us going and if we should keep going. But, think about it, would those we have lost want us to fail? With that in mind, would a significant other who cheated on us care if we failed—probably not, for now they have their own agenda. If it is a relative who has passed on, you better believe they are rooting for us from the other side! On the opposite hand, do we want that ex-significant other to fail too because they hurt us so deeply? That's debatable because they still may want to hurt us—and for a long time. Or, if it was our parent who died some time ago, we know deep down they would want us to continue living—and living to the fullest. Life is such a crapshoot sometimes, and I know I can't think of all the answers. How about you?

It's interesting to think about all the things that go through your mind when you're alone once again. You often wonder if there will ever be a new love that makes your heart skip a beat each time you see them. Their first glance at you is what you yearn for every day. Their arms around you for a much-needed hug helps melt away all your cares. I guess the statistics are correct when they say that it takes more muscles to frown than to smile, huh? But life can get to you sometimes to where you feel so lost. You feel that you are alone in this world and no one else can save you from your misery. You can also feel that you, alone, are the only one going through any type of trial in the world. Honestly, I think we are all in line awaiting that next test to assess our strength.

It seems like we are all at different points in our lives, but we all seem to match what happens to us at some point. We all deal with death, birth, success and failure, but it's the way we handle these circumstances that can make us triumph. Think of life this way, even as we age, so do our parents and acquaintances. But no one ever prepares us for our parent's passing—or anyone's passing.

Our next tragedy comes when we must make the decision to terminate our parents' life when it comes to a point of no return. They, as well as us, will get to their life's end where they cannot turn back. We must make sure they leave this world with dignity—it is our responsibility. But is letting them be removed from life support the best decision? Or would it be easier if they died from a heart attack with no one around who knows CPR? In either case, we are not mentally prepared to let them go. We will miss them, and we soon forget the sound of their voice. However, we will never forget those special times we shared with them. So, why is this information being compared to our demise? Well, the hurt from losing someone is comparable but not the same. Long story short, we're strong, but life's anguish seems to always be tapping us on our shoulder.

I guess we feel invincible sometimes to life's worries, but time waits for no one. However, time will come to prove us wrong and we are saddened by these events. Plus, the words of comfort we so desperately seek sometimes never come. These individuals will always be a part of us, but we must let them go just like our ex—who will never be a part of our lives like they once were. Just remember to look towards the Heavens for your answers and for your comfort when we feel there is no hope.

If we look back to our childhood and recall the conversations we had with our parents, relatives, and others, how do we feel about what was said? Were there words of hatred, or words expressing love and comfort? Our conversations showed what came from our heart—even though the words were hurtful or loving. That language judged us, and perhaps has followed us into our adulthood. Our tongue can be our friend, or it can be our enemy. Being able to control what we say is so important and no one can tell us to stop sometimes. For, our emotional state takes charge and controls our conversations. I know I've been there and once I get going, it's hard to stop. Those cogs in my head get geared up and the words come out of my mouth about my divorce and every other situation that has irritated me, and I usually regret what happens next. We try to take charge to control others at a particular moment, but we usually look silly in the process. Even years later our anger can take charge of our tongue, and we don't even realize it until it's too late. If we could only put a lock and key on that body part that talks too much, we could grow and learn by our past. Bringing our hatred into every situation, still, after years have passed, can bring us down. Just remember this, our tongue is a wet place where anything and everything can slip.

## 06.

## *H*old Me Tight and Make The Pain Go Away

Since that fateful day, I've noticed something that I hadn't noticed before. As I look in the mirror, I feel I have aged years beyond my physical age. I even look at my ex now and I see his salt and pepper hair, even more wrinkles, and serious health problems. As for me, I seem to color my hair every three weeks now, and each time I see someone go through the same misfortune, I ache. When circumstances keep piling on top of each other, I feel such heaviness on my chest; frustration in my soul, and my attitude of making it on my own is elevated. There are times when I need assistance from those around me, but sometimes I can't find it, or I don't want to ask. I just feel they have heard enough of my grief by this time.

*Attempting To Let Go*

When does life get better? When does that happiness gene come back and live inside me once again? Even the holidays don't help when it comes to being happy. Sure, all the promotion of the season is seen on TV, reiterated on the radio, and signs of "happiness" can be seen in store windows stressing "good cheer." Yeah, right! Wanting to be with family and friends—that you want to be with, that is the goal. Don't you agree? But, when family and friends don't live near you, where do you go next? Do we spend Thanksgiving, Christmas, and New Year's in our own cave? I remember last year I wanted to "cancel" Thanksgiving. If it weren't for my son, I would have done so. Those same feelings have come back to haunt me again this year. Knee surgery is once again scheduled for me and my friend's father is on his deathbed. I hate feeling this way. Even though I have my decorations up to celebrate these upcoming events, I guess I am just lost in the sparkle. Have I celebrated just for my son? I don't know, but I guess I'm just going with tradition to fit in for now.

As a child growing up, I guess I anxiously waited for Christmas to arrive. However, as each Christmas came and went, I never really got that special present that I longed to receive. After years of this, I realized as an adult that there was no need to wish for a certain gift. For, I knew it would never be given to me. To this day, I still feel this way. I have no desire to be disappointed once again. Another notch does not need to be put into the wall celebrating another botched event to disappoint me. I guess, sometimes, my negativity comes out too strong sometimes, although I really am a positive person. I try not to be consumed with negative feelings, but sometimes they conquer my thoughts in a very striking way. I guess one reason that the holidays bring them out in me, is that I have had three close relatives die, in different years, in the month of December.

Just think, this will be my second holiday season as a divorcee. Isn't this supposed to get easier as time passes? The need I have to be special in someone's life is still alive and well. It's got to be the same for everyone who is single and alone. Maybe it's our goal to be invincible to life's worries. But the time will come to prove us wrong, and we are saddened by these events. Perhaps we should look to the heavens for our much-needed answers—or at least for our own survival.

I guess the only tradition I need to follow around the holidays is the meaning they bring. Thanksgiving, to me, means being thankful for everyone and everything that I have in my life. Christmas means the birth of a Savior who will always be there for me— through the good and bad. I guess if we all looked at life with thankfulness, it wouldn't be all that bad, right? But what if we looked at someone else to give us that feeling of completeness? Perhaps we are just grabbing straws to find the longest, most sturdy one to prop us up until we can stand alone once again?

One thing that I've learned during this time of my life is that the "bad things" in life are out there, and others are quick to grab them to make your life miserable. Between significant others, former friends, and bosses, they may get to the point where they want to make you unhappy while pulling themselves upon a pedestal. They don't care about you for their mission is to create havoc, which makes us go through misfortune by their hand. Maybe I don't understand why people think the way they do—or is it that they must build themselves up while tearing other people down? Call me crazy, but I must question why people pull this crap?

Life is always handing us "challenges" on a platter and until it has passed, we ache. So, what do we do now? Well, I have learned that we must first lean on that man upstairs for we cannot veer away from the truth about life and living it to the fullest. Besides, the words to help us be in control of our life can come from the Bible. Words really do exist that we need to hear. But what God has done for us and how he is there when we really need him is something that isn't first to our mind, right?

When we won't let anyone help us because we don't want to be vulnerable, it is like continuing onward through a hurricane. The strong winds and heavy rain will only last for a specified amount of time, however, we will feel defenseless against a higher power and then the tragedy is revealed only at the end of the calm. It's the same as having a callus around your heart. Some may try to let others think they aren't affected by any misfortune. They won't allow anything to get through to them, and they cannot let any love in or out of their heart. Scary, huh? For now, there is no sensitivity to life in general.

Speaking of being sensitive to life. Haven't we all known someone who has been in a job for way too long? Their once helpful nature has been blackened with coal. There is no receptive nature for them to absorb any more positive thoughts and there is no need for them to be fulfilled by helping others. They are only there for a paycheck, and not to help those around them succeed. When others fail, no emotion exists. They don't care about anything anymore—they are only going through the motions. What has happened to people whose hearts and mind are tainted? Have they been desensitized to every emotion?

Perhaps it's like going back to an old relationship because you feel it is still ok to do so. Those old feelings are still a part of you that cannot be tossed aside, you have not buried those old emotions. But it didn't work then, and we just know it will never work in the future! Down deep, you know this! So, why would you even want to go back there again? When we are this low, do we just want a warm body to hold us tight? Perhaps we just want someone there for us and anyone will fit the bill until the right person shows up? Sometimes I should take my own advice!!

To go forward, a person must remember those emotions from their past, but you must walk away from them to clean your heart. Just think if your outside is clean, but not your inside, you may fall into that trap and return to what you wanted to run away from in the first place.

You must take care of yourself to keep you in balance, but first ask for help from God. Just think—if we feel no one is watching our actions, guess what, we sometimes do what we shouldn't? However, God knows exactly what we are doing; he also sees our day-to-day actions. Seeing our reflection in the mirror is a chore in itself. So, a good analogy of our daily lives would be to keep the inside of our cup clean, even though the outside may look spotless.

A person should not move into a new relationship to fulfill only himself or herself; they must take the other person into consideration before making that decision. For don't we need a relationship, founded on love and respect, so we will not be completely broken from the inside? We must also remember that the other half of us is just as important as that person we see when we look in the mirror. So, don't we all want to be treated like we treat others? But don't our friends and family sometimes scrutinize every part of life after we split from our ex? Do they take our side, or do they blame us? Sometimes, their concern seems to spill over into our existence so much so that it seems to choke us. But they only want the best for us, and guess what? We deserve it! We have been put through so much trying to get our lives back in order, and each trial seems to test our strength and knowledge of life. Why can't life be easier? Besides, it seems the older we get, the more Rubik cubes we are given to solve. I don't know about you, but I suck at that stupid game! I've seen people solve it in under a minute. As for me, it could be years before I could even get one side the same color unless I pull off the stickers and place them all on one side!

I recently watched a movie and in one part of it, I was dumbfounded. The topic of one conversation was, "When was the last time you were happy?" Wow! I looked back at my last 20 years in just a split second, and I could not pinpoint that specific time in my life. What happened to me? Did I base my life upon a relationship with a man I thought could make me happy? Or should I have been looking at my life in general? Have there been so few happy bits and pieces of my life, so miniscule, that I have forgotten them? Should the overall picture of my life been the one I should have looked for in the first place? I don't think I've been so astounded with one question in particular!

Right when I think I have moved on after my divorce, I am still finding that life can hit me so hard that I just want to cry myself to sleep once again. Then, I found out that the first guy I dated after my divorce now has another major medical issue. He really is a good person and now he is dealing with another thing he didn't ask for in his lifetime. He's going to be ok with some more medical treatment, and with all that has happened in his life, he still has a positive attitude. Even when his ex told him that no new woman would ever want him again, he trudged onward. He also had goals in his life that he has fulfilled. I guess life can be interesting to the point that what doesn't kill us makes us stronger, right? Sometimes I hate that saying, but it is so true. Plus, each time I jump over another hurdle, I feel that I have accomplished a bit more of my time on this earth. I suppose life isn't all that bad.

I guess I have one question about "Life" now. Why do we sometimes retreat into that "black hole" when we think we have to deal with tragedy by ourselves? I've seen it so abundantly lately in people and they seem to have acquired duct tape over their mouths because they won't speak about it. In my case, I have "diarrhea of the mouth" when I'm stressed and overloaded. Perhaps I just need to vent to relieve my anxiety. On the other hand, I've seen so many men, and women, run the other direction and not let anyone help them. Why? Have they always handled life in this manner because they feel no one is there for them? Are they embarrassed that their life is falling apart? Who knows. Even if people volunteer their services of comfort to their friends and family who so desperately need it, they can be rejected. I know I am usually the first one in line when my friends need emotional support. I want to give them a hug, say words of comfort, and tell them I am available at the end of their telephone when they need to vent.

Was it my upbringing or my military service that formed my emotions? Who knows! I just know that I feel their pain even though it's not my own. I even flinch when I see someone get a shot with a needle. I guess I'm hard-wired that way for my emotions weigh heavily on my shoulder—and all the time. I even have a hard time understanding why a person retreats into a world of their own, for days and sometimes years, and doesn't want to deal with anyone. Perhaps they think that since they are not vocal, that the people around them will just leave them alone until they come out of that black hole. That kind of thinking just breaks my heart. I want to be there for them, and I don't understand why they don't want me there. Maybe it's the way they are hardwired on the ways of everyday life.

I recently had an experience where a friend lost his father. He retreated, after the funeral, for three days to sleep and decompress. I was worried about him for not asking for my support, but he assumed that I would just leave him alone until he was ready to appear again. Say what? This caused a conflict between us, because neither of us understood the other's thinking.

Is it just men who don't want to deal with an emotional crisis? Well, I'm sure there are some women out there with the same thinking. Plus, were little boys raised to hold back their tears and "man up" when they are crushed? So then, why do fathers comfort their daughters when tears are so prevalent? I don't want to raise my son to always be that way. I want him to shed those tears when sadness consumes him. I want him to understand that getting out his feelings of loss and defeat is healthy for his soul.

If we lend ourselves to our children and be sensitive to their needs, we will grow an adult who understands life a little better, right? We can only hope. I guess we need to wash ourselves out from the inside, for those words and feelings to come out and be present to others. We must remember that there is no fear in loving, for a "perfect" love will cast our fears.

Now that years have past since we had that "divorce monkey" on our backs, are we still a loving person? Have we become hateful in our acts regarding our new relationships? Are we still afraid of getting too close to another person because it may one day hurt us? Do we now jump from one relationship to another because we're not comfortable with just one mate? Plus, does commitment scare us to the point that we run in the other direction? I know it's crossed my mind a time or two. It just seems that we are so cautious now and we are so afraid of being happy that we are making ourselves very miserable. Or are we just avoiding the inevitable situation that will happen on a future date? I've even seen people put all their energy into their immediate family, and now they can have an "escape clause" to get out of a relationship. They could choose to be happy in their personal life, but they choose not to be with someone who completes them. Why does a person put others first and themselves last? I guess if we knew how others thought, we'd be ahead of the game, huh? I just wish I could get that flipping crystal ball fixed, so I knew these answers!!

As for me, I don't think I will ever understand men—they probably don't understand me either. Plus, isn't it quite inevitable that both sexes seem to think quite differently? Men, if you're reading this right now, you're probably thinking the same thing! I guess I think this way because I've been hurt so badly in the past. It may be the fact that sometimes I never deal with those past feelings. Well, maybe. I guess some events make me wonder why people try to run and hide behind new people and experiences. I've even seen some men work themselves to death to escape their woos while others try to put another notch on their bedpost for another "female" conquest or vice versa. Say what? I guess we need to evaluate our past because it sometimes seems that we repeat our wrongs and never really break out of that pattern. Remember, a great runner never turns around to see where they have been. They only deal with the obstacles they encounter on the way to their destination by looking forward to the finish line. Considering this thought, our past can hinder our future, but only if we let it.

We must always remember if we look back at our past, the "should haves," "would haves," and "could haves" will always haunt us. So, if we can't see our past for what it was—a lesson learned—we cannot move forward. Just like in our elementary and high school days, we had experiences where we were given not so nice nicknames. I know I had a few that really traumatized me. As I now look back, those painful memories are still there, but I don't deal with them on a daily, hourly, or weekly basis. I have toughened my soul to deal with those "childish" pranks. I guess it was a good lesson for my adulthood.

Who knows why we go through the stresses that we do, but they're there. I don't like it anymore than the next person, but I refuse to let it break me. So, how do we get out of that rut in life? One way is to write those feelings down on paper and just take a glance at it. Just review all the good and bad that have happened to us, and what we have "dished out." People can't take back the wrongs against others, but they can learn from it. Consider this, it's like a debt paid in full. God did this for us too—the price of our sins was and still is taken away by him—everyday.

As we look back at our life in a nutshell, can we see that love keeps no record of wrongs? Think of life like this—when we are in a relationship and we constantly bring up past events that made us mad about our significant other, how does it make us feel—or even them? Do we want to be reminded of how and what we did to cause a fight six months ago? I know I don't want that! I'm not perfect and neither are any of my past significant others in my life. So, are we walking in hate because we can't move onward? Sounds like it, huh?

Our pain is something that will never go away—think about it. We will always have a memory of those bad times even though an era has muffled the pain. I guess it's like having gone through childbirth; women remember how uncomfortable it was, but the actual pain is no longer present. We know it existed, and we knew it hurt terribly, but the ultimate outcome was a new beginning. From then on, we have conquered each event, and each triumph has been that victory we needed to survive. Can you say, "Exit Stage Right?"

Just like watching our children grow, we have grown ourselves. We pick them up when they fall and care for the wounds they sustain. We really could learn by caring for our children, for they are our strength to go on. Setting an example for them by our actions shows them how they can overcome their fears. Our strength can be theirs; we must set a goal to find it.

## 07.

## *The Next Chapter of Me*

Since the beginning of time, couples as well as friends, have had disagreements. Some relationships have stood the test of time in their battles; others have lost the conflict and split away from each other. As for a friend of mine, Julia, she first married in 1956. Yes, her years in this lifetime are many, but her words of wisdom really amazed me. She was only married nine years, but they were eventful years. Her divorce was uncontested even though her ex cheated on her. The settlement consisted of her being awarded $100 a month for child support (for two children) by the court system. The irony of it all was that she had to go after their dad to pay! Sounds a little cruel huh? She had to know where he was working and when he was paid to get these funds. She ended up going to court for a second time, and the judge basically told her that he didn't want to see her in his court room ever again. Hello? What did he just say?

A man's world was so obvious then, and women had to fight for everything. As Julia put it, "It was a man's world, and men protected men." So, the "norm" was while men prospered after a divorce, women went on welfare! What a difference 30 to 40 years have now made! Currently, the norm is for the county government to go after that dead-beat parent. Another interesting fact about Julia's predicament was that if the parent applied for a fishing license back then, the state had a way to find that parent who had to pay child support, because the state now had the information to locate them—strange huh?

Julia's story started just as many have—her first husband cheated on her, which caused a lot of heartache. It literally put her into the hospital from emotional distress. When she first found out about her husband's actions, she immediately got sick and vomited. Wow! This news came out of nowhere and she was thrown for a loop—she eventually had to move out of her home so she could progress forward. Some people seem to handle change better than others, but when change hits you this hard, it's not easy to regroup. Believe me, I know!

To this day, she cannot even remember how long it took her to get over him. As I discussed this difficult period with her, I could still see how she still "loved" that man whom she first married. However, it was also that same "man" who left her dangling from a cliff, and it is still a mystery why did what he did. But she said she finally got to a point where she grew stronger and stronger with each passing day. Being once at the bottom of a precipice, she gained the strength to pull herself up, so she never had to look back. Years later when she encountered him again, she realized that his life did not grow into something positive—he was the same person who first said goodbye to her. He was still the arrogant and selfless man who had cheated on her. Guess he didn't learn anything, huh?

I suppose it was a total shock to her, that as a couple, they had spent so much time together, but he chose to commit adultery with a bar maid—literally! Even his friends held his horrid secret for him the whole time. That brotherhood really existed back then—but does it really exist now? Perhaps. But who is loyal to anyone anymore? Marriage is such a "throw-away" habit today. Even back then, TV shows such as *"Leave It To Beaver," and "Father Knows Best"* really had meaning. But, in the shadows of those TV programs there was hurt that was never shown in public—on and off the screen.

As years passed, she decided to stay single, why? Her reasoning was, "Why wouldn't you?" She now had her schedule in place as a single parent. She even made her major decisions by writing the pros and cons down on a piece of paper. She was "It" and all her life's decisions revolved only around her. It was her realization that if she were married once again, she would be doing everything for "him" and her family—and not for herself. Having her own independence was an important part of her life now, and she didn't want to give it up.

Giving and taking is an important part of any new relationship, but how was she going to find it? She never knew at any point that any man could be the right one with which to share her life. Because, even if we live with that special person for any length of time, and then get married, will it last? Sometimes the answer is "yes," but many other times it could be "no." What is it that waits to be revealed that never shows up while anyone is dating a person? Boy, I wish I knew that answer!!

It was nine years later, and even though Julia wasn't looking for a relationship, she met her second husband. He first impressed her because he had two boys for which he was seeking custody. His actions totally took her by surprise, and she was smitten by his caring actions. She appreciated the fact that he took charge and wanted to be a good dad. They were compatible and she "liked" him. Did I miss something? She "liked" him! Humm—shouldn't that expression be one of love? That was my reaction when she told me about him. Did this start only with respect, and not that deep down love that needs to blossom into a relationship? Gee, I could be wrong—well, that would be a gigantic, Yikes!

As for this relationship, it too, did not last long. It was almost like a *"Brady Bunch"* story—she had two kids; he had two kids. The only problem was that his kids had different rules than her kids—in his mind, anyway. His way of thinking eventually broke them apart after another nine years of "wedded bliss." It's strange that the "nine"-year point was her ultimate demise once again. Plus, she let me know that she didn't "divorce" her second husband; she divorced "his" son. Just think they had four teenagers in their household at once. Boy, that many teenagers, every other week, that's a lot! I couldn't imagine the hormones that were flowing freely in that home!

So, let's try to understand something about life. We are born, we learn to crawl, followed by elementary and high school, getting our independence at 18 years of age, and then college or a job? Does society pressure us to get married just because that's what our parents expect of us? But, if we don't get married, what happens then? Are we failures in life? On another note, what does our sexual preference say of us? If we don't fit that mold that mom and dad placed us in all those years ago, are we not accepted by society? There are a lot of questions for which we may never get the answers we so desperately need. Think of it this way, love is a gamble any way we look at it. So, should we lead, follow or get the hell out of the way from our emotions? One thing we can perhaps do is bet on a special someone that we meet after our divorce and just hope that all the pieces fall together. Occasionally, the timing isn't right, and we let each other go for some crazy reason. If this happens, should we get out of this rat race for good? We all long for that special person to return to us, but at what cost? Life never seems to reveal the reasons why things happen to us, but we must be thoroughly aware of them when they happen. It's what we do with the information that will ultimately comfort us or tear our life apart—once again.

Ok, I've shared one opinion about life, love and getting on with it. My next story is about Susan. I've known her for many years, and I've seen her struggle desperately in several relationships. She states that she really didn't get a handle on love—from an early age. Susan was the youngest of four siblings and the last one left at home. She told me that she felt very isolated because all she saw between her parents was violence. Her goal was to escape from her reality. Reading hardback books about storybook romance, that many girls so desperately desire, was what she thought life was all about. She really believed it existed since back then; the man worked, and the woman stayed home and raised the children. No one ever cheated on his or her soul mate and life was perfect. Not! Like so many, her dream world did not exist, and reality hit her when she was just a teenager.

With no one to share her plan to "escape" from reality, she thought her only recourse was to get pregnant, so that her parents would let her marry the future father of her baby. After executing her arrangement, her parents were furious. For, they just knew she was making a grave mistake because she was just 16 years old. Pregnancy was her first oversight. Then she added a marriage certificate to a situation that was bound for failure. Ouch! On top of this whole mess that the two of them created on purpose, all three of them eventually lived with his parents! Can you say, "adding insult to injury?"

She can look back now and think what a horrid decision she made in just a short period of time. The only good thing that came out of this whole mess was her son. Her little bundle of joy was her whole world, but was he a burden to her in some way? She wasn't even old enough to legally have a drink, and now she has a baby that depended solely on her! Besides, this relationship was doomed from the beginning. It wasn't based on a love relationship, just an affiliation outside of her parent's home. If you think this relationship lasted, you're wrong; only six months passed until her beginning became her end.

Adding misfortune to more tragedy was the next scenario. After leaving Husband #1, she and her son moved back into her mom's house. Sometime during this mess, her dad also died, so now she was living back in an environment very similar to the one she left. Plus, another family member moved into her mom's house, and the violence persisted. Now she had a child, was "alone: once again, and was still looking for that romance she just knew existed. She deserved a happy life, but where would she find it?

Enter Husband #2, from Stage Left, or from her church— that is. Just a few years had passed since she left her first husband. However, she was still naïve about men and how relationships worked. Since this guy went to church, she "assumed" that he would be the perfect one—once again, she was confused about how love worked. She thought that if this guy "loved" God with all his heart, he was the one, right? Can you say NO! This one did drugs! Yes, he was on drugs. Say what? So, she left him. Then, her mother tried to talk her into going back to him after she found out that her daughter had left another relationship! Did her mother understand the situation? From what I understand, I don't believe so. But it was only after a major fight between her and her mom that made Susan leave her mother's home and return to Hubby #2. Nothing changed when she returned, but this situation was better than living with her mom. There was no respect from this guy, did she expect any? Maybe not. But, by leaving her mother's house, she was just trying to escape another situation that made her unhappy. She did, however, get a little satisfaction later. His cousins had a "blanket" party for him, and he was the main course.

At this point her son was four years old. She had no transportation, no admiration from her husband, and felt there was nowhere to go. Once again, many thoughts ran through her mind. She didn't know what her future held, and she didn't know what to do next or how to do it. She yearned for something better, but how do you get from Point A to Point B without a plan of action? She had no clue! It seemed that she was with her "interim partner," and not her soul mate. Was there a period where she thought it would work? Who knows? For, she had gotten married a very short time after her first relationship, and now she had a son whose "father" was not his own. So, what did her son think of this new relationship? He was barely out of the toddler stage, and now he had a new dad. What kind of impression was his brain storing? What part of this current life would stay with him into adulthood?

Kids are very resilient when it comes to tragedy, but they never forget those tender moments that change their way of thinking. Believe me, I've been there. I revisit those moments occasionally, but I try not to stay there—it's too depressing to be there for too long. I have grown from it, I don't want to relive those moments, and I don't let it consume me. For, when you're a child, how much of an education about life do you really have so you can deal with tragedy? Plus, is your family's financial situation and where you live, in addition to the current year you experience these events, have a lot to do with your current situation? I think it really does.

At this point another change was about to occur. You probably won't believe this, but Husband #2 was history only months after their turbulent relationship. Once again, her personal life was in turmoil for she had failed again in her mission to pursue a perfect life. She was still looking for that love she so desperately wanted and a stable home for her son. She decided to move out on her own, but again, she would struggle. She concluded that to survive she must be married—say what? I could only imagine what she was thinking since her alternate plan was to have another marriage certificate on her side table. It was about six months later and, guess what? Husband #3 came into her life. Once again, she was looking for security. She did not "love" him; but she did "like" him. Once more she was looking for love in all the wrong places and for all the wrong reasons. She met this new guy in a parking lot after asking for directions. I guess we meet people in a lot of different situations, but in a parking lot? I guess I shouldn't judge; I once met and went out with a guy that I met at a car wash! Yikes, what was I thinking?

This time Susan was looking for something different. Her son had been in therapy after the second divorce and since the counselor suggested a stable home, that was now her goal. Gee, isn't that what we all want—a stable environment?

Unfortunately, our kids seem to get the worst backlash from their parents splitting. They, like us, evaluate every situation or even the people who caused the split, but they are left to deal with the consequences. Now her son had another man who influenced his mother and himself. What was going through his little mind?

Susan seemed to have a life that started out in a home with issues that didn't deal with loving ways. Then she was delusional about the "fairy tale" romance that she continually searched for, for so many years. She admitted to me that she never loved any of her three husbands. Wow! Life for her had to be sad for years for her to admit these lies that she told herself. It seems her only goal in life was to "survive" and to do it the best way possible. I still admire her spirit!

It was Susan's third marriage that was quite eventful. Not only did she have a son from her first husband, but also as time passed, she had a daughter with her third husband. Both of her kids were constantly fighting, but life did get a little easier. This time she felt she was smarter about marriage. She now had the confidence to demand a higher criterion in the man she wanted. Being more aware of what she wanted, what a man could offer, and not putting up with any more crap was at the top of her list. Even though this one lasted for several years, alas, a divorce was looming around the corner.

Those same emotions came into play for her when circumstances beyond her control told her to leave this relationship too.

After her third divorce, Susan's daughter rebelled. She did not know of the circumstances involved in her parents' breakup, but she blamed her mother for abandoning her, since her mom moved out. Now her parents were split apart, because her mother had left the home and had got a job in a town several miles away. It was very hurtful to her daughter, but Susan could not reveal those issues that made it impossible to continue their "marriage." Her daughter dealt with her hurt by being around animals, for they did not judge her. They appreciated her for whom she was—not for what they wanted her to be or become. However, all her emotions were eventually healed with furry critters that can't speak the English language.

I guess we could all learn from her actions. Susan had her reasons to leave this man, and they were quite legitimate, but she wanted to explain to her daughter why she left her dad, but she couldn't. The only reason I can reveal is that it dealt with money. In the divorce agreement, Susan didn't fight him with that issue—she wanted him to have money to help raise their daughter.

You've probably guessed by now that, yes, she did get married for the fourth time! The scary thing is that she's still married after 14 years. I'm not kidding! The old saying goes, "three times a charm." For her it was the fourth time. After marriage "number three," she was determined to find a relationship to last for the rest of her life. This time she admitted that she knew exactly what she wanted; even though she thought husband #3 was going to be the "one." Number four was out there somewhere and when she met him, he had been single for 22 years. She stood back and viewed him as no one before. She looked at how he carried himself around his family. However, he was very depressed when they first met because of the goals he set out for himself—to retire happy—it was not met. For, his spouse died before this could be accomplished. Susan even knew his wife, which was another strange twist in this relationship. Things just seemed to click and fall into place. Was she at the right place at the right time? She thinks so, for he was at his wits end and he was discouraged with life—still sounds strange, huh? Well, keep reading.

Their relationship started off as friends—not as a convenient situation. They first got to know each other at Thanksgiving, and by spending a lot of time together. Wow! What happened? Did she finally learn from all her failed relationships and false hopes that now she really did know what she wanted? Well, now he is husband #4.

She admitted to me that her current husband finally taught her what love was, but there is no magic pill to get that fairy tale to materialize. It takes work to be in "love" with someone and it takes two individuals working hard to keep that magic in a relationship. It's only after you step back from a connection that you truly understand your feelings. Are we all in a situation where security is our only goal in life? Do we have to have that new shiny car or that big house to feel that you've "made it" in life? Or is it important just to have a feeling of accomplishment that makes us tick?

Susan's story began in the 70s, and now it's 2010. She has a way to share her feelings now that she didn't before. She even admitted to me that her parents were against everyone she ever dated. Perhaps she wanted to sow her "wild oats" to show them she could accomplish whatever she set out to do? Perhaps her failed marriages were the result of her lack of understanding about how a real relationship should work? For there were 14 years that passed between her first, second, and third marriages! Ouch! I was married for almost 20 years to the same idiot, and I didn't leave, she had three idiots to deal with, and when it wasn't working, she left! I could have taken lessons from her. Just think of all the grief we both went through, but it could have been avoided! She had more stamina than I ever had.

Each century has its different dress, different lifestyle, and different way of thinking. We can challenge these things, but do we ever win? Plus, can we even find what we're looking for when we don't even know what we're looking for or where it's even located? Life is such a mystery sometimes and things can happen to totally put a fork in the road to make us take a detour. This detour in life may be one in which we don't choose for ourselves. Events happen, whether they are planned or not, they happen, and usually we make our next decisions from these occasions.

I'm also reminded of a time, just a few years back, when my son was younger. He did something that now makes me think about life in general. I bought a loaf of French bread to have with our meal one night. I cut the end piece of the bread for me and another one for my son. I continued to fix dinner, and after my ex arrived home, he saw the bread on the counter. He reached for the bread to get cut a piece for himself, and then he realized that my son had hollowed out the "soft" part of the bread and then left the shell. He was somewhat upset after telling me to look at what was left; however, we both had a good laugh. My son had taken the part that was easily accessible and tasted the best part, and then left the rest that he thought wasn't good enough for him.

As I look back now, I see that times in our life can feel like a "hollow shell," but only if we let it. If all the original parts of something are gone, we must realize that we are afforded the opportunity to fill it back up once again. But we can only do this if we set our minds to it. Right? If we let an opportunity go by and do nothing, what are we proving to ourselves—that we want others to feel sorry for us? Do we cheat to fill ourselves up and only ourselves? Or do we step up to the plate and do something to change our position? Our thinking can last for only a short while or it can last for a lifetime. Personally, I want the latter; I know that I don't want anyone to feel sorry for me—ever! Maybe it's the fact that it takes too much out of a person to feel sorry for them. Perhaps it's the fact that I appear stronger than others; in reality, I have the same hurt that others have when they have been destroyed by a relationship. Being knocked off your feet hurts—especially if you hit your head!

It seems the hurt never really goes away. Every Thanksgiving and each Christmas still has the stigma of the hurt I first felt. Sure, there were good feelings at one time, oh so long ago. But it seems after a divorce, all we have in our heart are the feelings that first caused us harm. When we revisit them, we ache all over. Only television shows that we knew in childhood seem to put a smile on our face. Unfortunately, it only lasts for a short while. Remember when the Flintstones, Snoopy, and Miracle on 34th Street put a smile on our heart? When I revisit that time of my life, I felt happy, but it's short-lived.

Looking back to my childhood, I remember growing up and then moving out of my parent's home. Reality seemed to set in and the fairy tale that we once knew as a child seems so far away. I guess everything we want in life can be a little scary on how to get it, especially if we want it so badly. But, finding that soul mate is such a chore sometimes. Then we find out that person wasn't meant to be with us to the day we die. Needless-to-say, a divorce is never easy, but how do we peel off the tough layers and begin anew? I just know that I want to stop falling and finally touch the bottom. Maybe then I will be able to pick up myself and start climbing to the top again.

## 08.

## Where Do I Go From Here

Now tell me this, why do people, both men and women, get divorced and then look back at those memories as failure. Then, they try to prove something to themselves by NEVER getting married again. On the other hand, when a person wants their life to begin once more, when do they say, "enough is enough," and start drastically looking for Mr. or Ms. Right to fill them up? Plus, what is their reasoning for either choice? We're all afraid to take that step again, and when a new relationship stares us in the face, do we choose to run? Or do we look at it from afar, and then get closer to the point that we can release the reins of our heart once again?

We all want to be held closely; we want to be told we're special and that we matter to someone. I think this is what we call our "soul mate?" This person is there for us through thick and thin and they never want to let us go. For, they can't stand to be out of our sight—and vice versa. Is this all a bunch of crap or what? I guess it depends on how our brain has been wired. How important is it for us to have a person in our lives once again—for they may or may not hurt us?

If a person chooses to never get married again, what are their reasons? Are they so content in their own skin that they do not have any more room in their hearts, nor in their home, for another warm body? Do they not want to be "bothered" with a person who can turn their life upside down from their current situation? Have they not let go of those hurt feelings they were handed by their significant other all those years ago. What state of mind do they now hold so precious? Where do we go from the wounds that have suffocated our heart? When do we let go of the hurt that has haunted us for so long? These are difficult questions that only we can answer, or can we? We can get advice from our friends and family who have our best interests in mind, but do we ever listen?

It's only when we're ready to move onward that we take that first step. However, do we look back for that former "soul mate" to be waiting in the wings to take you back, if they have once handed you your freedom? Think of it this way, when a couple is together, but life pulls them apart, how can they make things work? Where is the trust factor with a new person, if the feelings you once had now have disjointed you, and on more than one occasion? Plus, if your life is still revolving around the earth while that significant others life has stopped, what's next? There are so many confusing circumstances that we must all face; it's what we do with those feelings that determine our future. But, if we are lucky enough to find the one, we want to start our life with again, don't we want it to start right away?

Finding the "one" we want to spend forever with seems so difficult sometimes. Plus, if we're just dating someone just for the sake of having someone to fill the void in our lives, what are we proving to ourselves? We must learn that the next time around, we shouldn't just put up with a person to include everything they do to irritate us, just to have someone in our bed. We must get the strength to get rid of that terminally ill romance—for it will not make us happy. We are just going through the steps of pure lust—not true love. There are just so many questions we must ask ourselves, and that person, to make sure we are headed in that straight and narrow direction. I guess it's a way of thinking, which we either desire more money in our lives to fulfill our earthly needs or we use what's in our heart to make more memories.

We must remember that evil can interrupt our lives and pollute our world. Not getting rid of ignorance around us can infiltrate our soul and our planet. It can also make us wake up one morning and not know where we have gotten to today, which could occur in a very short time. Just keep in mind, when we are at the bottom of our existence, our life can become anew. Just like a sprout growing for the first time after a fire. We must plan our future and bury our past—for ashes can surround us and we don't even know it. We have a responsibility to ourselves for our new existence to begin.

Just thinking we can make changes in our life without the help of a higher power is a little ridiculous—in my opinion. I know that when my heart aches—and to this day. Through each holiday that was once filled with a family, the feelings and emotions of a "family" are not there any more which makes me know that I am not thoroughly healed. I long for a feeling of belonging to a "family unit" once again. I also need God to be in my life to escape the hurt that still lingers. Making decisions based on your dignity and intelligence, to define whom you are, will ultimately define us on how well we rise after we have fallen.

Years after a divorce we are all different. We have grown, been down to the bottom of the barrel with our distraught emotions and sometimes hate life in general. There are several things that I have learned since my divorce. I now know that I need to give God the first and best of everything that I can offer. I need to thank him for everything that I now have and will have in the future and remember not to give him the leftovers of me. I need to finish what I start for where I was going was a dead end. I need to turn back and be concerned what God would want for me. For, he has given me more than I could ever repay; I need to give thanks to him always.

It's almost like that old saying that everything happens for a reason. I see it every day at my job. The tragedies happening to families all around me just seem to make me think that those family units were not to be. Maybe it's the Holy Spirit who is at work cleaning up the mess that never should have happened. Perhaps a sense of empowerment is taking place in those faces I see day in and day out. Whatever the reason, I give them advice and send them on their way. I often wonder if they really survive as they let the door close behind them; I can only hope. My wish for them is for God to reveal himself to them so they can make their life right. We all need a higher power just to get through the day sometimes; remember that ok?

I have so many friends and acquaintances that have been married for a long time, and some have been divorced for several years and/or remarried. An observation I made involves the ones who have been divorced for a very long time. They seem content in their lives. They don't want to be bothered with a person whom they think will change their being—since their "life" is currently what they want. I really wonder if a person is destined to be alone for the rest of their life. Another person I know will not go out with anyone unless certain criteria is met—and they are standing by their guns on this one. Sometimes when a person is burned by a relationship, they will never compromise ever again. Their next soul mate has to conform to their ways, or they turn their head and walk the other direction. Some put up with the same crap for a while and then finally blow up because they're in the same kind of bond they just left. Wow! We are such creatures of habit—or in this case—NOT!

Now the question is where is our comfort zone? After a divorce, a person can be bitter with their life, avoid relationships, or swear off any "significant other" forever. In the case of a death, we can be sad for eternity because our soul mate has died without our permission. So, since we never want to feel that dread again, we now have a reason to be single until the day we check out. Think of life this way. With every little noise we hear in our home that never bothered us before, now becomes an issue—just like that "bad" relationship. But, getting someone to share our bed—whom we can nudge to check out that noise—isn't a priority anymore. Even if we were light sleepers, and our special someone snored so loud that it woke up the dead, we now can't sleep at all. Even doing things as a couple that you once enjoyed, such as building a fire in the fire pit outside, may make us calm. But it doesn't fill us up as much as we need. There's still something missing, but we can't figure it out. However, we are still hesitant to find that missing link, right?

As each day goes by, life seems to change piece by piece. Each holiday, each weather event, and each happening thereafter where your "prior" significant played an event, can still haunt you. Remember when he or she was there to cook, clean, mow the grass, shovel the snow, or wash the car? Now, it's just you. So, have you counted the days, months and years that you have been alone without a special someone in your life? Well guess what? You're the one who does everything now. You have no one to help you unless you can convince your friends, neighbors and family that you're desperate. So, how long will you put up with that list of things that you don't want to do? Or, if you look back at your prior life, did you do all those things anyway, so it's not such a big deal now? That's the way I felt when I was with my ex. I cooked, cleaned, vacuumed, mowed the grass, shoveled the snow, did the laundry, cut and stacked the firewood, and ironed. In addition, I was "full-time" mom. What the Hell was I thinking? I let him get away so much that my friend, Marie, was mad at him! She was probably mad at me for letting him get away with it. What was I to do? He was out fooling around, and had an excuse for why he couldn't help me—he was busy working! Yeah, right! I try not to go to that unhappy place, but occasionally for about five minutes, I slip into that hole. So, I try not to dwell on those events in my life, or I'd really be angry—and for a very long time.

We can look back at the events in our life and wonder why we did the things we did, or we can learn from them and move on. With the beginning of each new year, we can reflect back on what worked and what didn't. We can only learn those lessons now and progress towards our wants, desires, and needs. Each challenge can get us to think about what our next move will be and how we can accomplish it. Will we look back at the past year and wonder if the path we are currently on will be our ultimate future? Or is our goal to change where we are heading and find another dream? Will we look at what we thought we didn't want last year and now desire it with all our heart? Plus, it's sometimes hard to figure out if we messed up our chances at a new chance to be with a new special someone. If we want them back, how will we do it now? Has our mindset changed to the point where we can convince them to come back to us? Or have we lost that opportunity?

The lessons learned from our mistakes from New Year's Day to the end of December can take us to places we never thought of before. Besides, each year don't we look back and wish things were different in one way or another? There just seems to not be any answer to our questions in life. We must evaluate where we are now, and where we want to be in a certain amount of time. Plus, each year brings another birthday to our existence, and time stands still for no one, especially us. We must understand that what we don't participate in today may or may not be available for us tomorrow. We can toss aside the things we don't want to deal with, but they may come back to haunt us. I know that with each passing day, the hurt of divorce has subsided for me. However, it never seems to go away, but why would we want it to haunt us forever? There will still be things in that "past" marriage that we can't let go of, but we must learn that we don't want to repeat it. The hurt, the anger, and the frustration may be tucked deep down inside our soul to the point that we don't want to deal with it, nor do we want to speak of it.

Getting those feelings out of our heart must be a goal. I guess I can compare it to our military members who were in Vietnam. To this day, they have hurt, tragedy, and remorse that they can never speak of with their spouse. Then they were treated badly when they came home—but they were only doing their job. Thank goodness, we as Americans have learned that we enjoy our freedom from those who have fought for it. I can understand this because I too, am a military veteran.

This close "family" unit that is thrust upon a person never goes away when one leaves the military. The old saying, "once a Marine; always a Marine," is as true as any other branch of the service. Besides, it seems that once a person admits (in a conversation) that they are a veteran, the "brotherhood" spills out and they could talk for hours of the "sea stories" they shared. I have found that veterans can talk and talk about anything—even though they just met. It's too bad that this bond sometimes cannot exist in marriages and relationships.

Recently I met a lady who was totally turned upside down at one point in her life. Not only was she in turmoil because she had a controlling ex-husband, but she had lost her job, and she had medical issues to top it all off. I can't imagine what she went through since she compared him to the movie, *"Sleeping With The Enemy."* She told me she was constantly afraid for her life and for her kids, because in his eyes, she couldn't do anything right—ever! At the point where I met her, years had past and she had left her husband, her children were grown, and she had married her high-school sweetheart. Wow! With all the information she told me about the crises in her life, I was surprised she made it to this point. I did, however, feel her strength through her words of wisdom.

The calm in her voice and the poise she reflected on was enough to make me believe that we can all make a life for ourselves that will work. It's what's in our heart and our stamina that can get us to that next "happy" relationship. It's always surprising to note that no one ever wants to be in a bad relationship, but we always seem to find that one person who changes our mind. I know I've had enough of those relationships that I never want another one. The only good that can come from them is the fact that we learn valuable lessons that can never be found anywhere else. We just must figure out how to get out in the first place.

Now that we've covered women whose lives were torn apart because of a disastrous relationship, getting a man's perspective is now in order. My friend, James, also has a history of relationships that went awry. He's been married twice, and both times his wives cheated on him. It's now the year 2011; he's been divorced since 1991. So, why hasn't he taken the plunge once again? Is it that his trust was broken so badly that he can't, nor he won't go "there" again? He and other divorced men that I've known really don't want to talk about their past. They just "suck it up" and go on about their day.

No wonder men die first—they don't use the art of "diarrhea of the mouth," and nothing comes out of that tear duct gland in their eyelids! Think about it. Men, in general, close their mouth and their hearts to pain that they can't control. Most were raised to believe that they should suppress their feelings and never let another person see their frailties. They are to be "strong" in every way and never weak. Ouch! Who came up with those ideas? In James' case, his last marriage, he became the victim of distance because they were too far away from each other.

Then the nuptials became less of a priority as time wore on. He informed me that when men get burnt, they become more careful. If they see a commitment coming at them, they will run, and after some time. I guess their memory can become very fresh because they keep it in a little part of their heart where they can grasp it too easily. Becoming ready for a new relationship is never a priority in their lives. All the pieces need to fall into place, but sometimes the timing is off. There can't be any sickness, money, or any other issues that would traumatize the relationship to doom it to failure. But, as James said, a man gets to a point where they don't want to be alone. But what will they eventually change in their lives to get to that point? Is it their age that changes their frame of mind? Is it the fact they come home to a big house with no one to greet them except for the dog? Whatever rationale they use, their past can always hurt them, but only if they let it.

No matter the reason, men really do have a giving heart—whether or not they know it or even want to admit it. They want to be the "strong" person in a relationship, but they also require the softness of a partner. I'm right, aren't I? Girlfriend, you know it! James went on to tell me that most relationships don't work because, in his case, he couldn't give any relationship what he wanted. Between his work and family obligations, his associations suffered. Say what? Shouldn't we be there to help our family and friends, but also make time for our own life? I know that if a person constantly takes care of everyone else, they are the ones who suffer in the end. I've been there; it's not a friendly place to be. Besides, when this happened in the past, his relationships were lost. Not only were both of his marriages affected, but also his dating relationships have suffered since. So, after being in a relationship that should have worked—and most recently—he never committed himself wholly to that person. Did his past come back to haunt him once more? Besides, when does one realize that their life could become happy, but only if they relax their heart muscles?

Well, after being consumed last year with tragic issues that affected him personally, he is now ready to "settle" down with someone on a permanent basis. He feels that he is at a point in his life, he wants to share his bed and his life with a special someone. He wants to welcome that special person with dinner and a kiss when they come through the door. He is grasping for that relationship he once had, but will he get the opportunity to rekindle it? Only time will tell, for that relationship he once held so dear, but kept so far away, may only be a memory in his past. He is hoping his life will get to the point where he is "truly" happy—and for the rest of his life. I wish him well in his endeavors, he deserves happiness.

It seems as I write this book all I can find is one disastrous divorce or separation after another. Well, guess what? Today is no different—I found another one. Today I learned that one of my former co-workers is separated from her husband. When I heard this, my heart began to weep. She has been through so much in her life—in the four years that I've known her. Her son had gotten into some trouble with the police a couple of years back and is now incarcerated. Her soon-to-be ex-husband, in this timeframe, broke his back, leg, and was severely injured on his job, and has had two knee replacements. Her finances are minimal, her house is for sale, her soon-to-be ex is between jobs, and her spirit is broken.

Once again, I feel "that" heaviness that once engulfed me when I was going through my divorce. I felt her burdens and her grief. She is a very strong person, but a strong person can be knocked off their pedestal if enough events happen to rattle their world. Sometimes life's actions make me wonder if they're really caused by one's actions or someone else's. Did I, or another person, do something to make my life so miserable now? Perhaps. However, I don't think any one person asks for this much grief—ever! She is a good person. Her family has been through so much, and yet more heartache seems to appear out of nowhere. Can she make it? I certainly hope so, because I've seen some of my other friends in similar situations. They were strong through the storm, and now their life has made a 360-degree turn. It just makes me so sad to see these events happen. If only we could see our future events, for they may not happen since we could prevent them with our current position.

To this day I still wonder why things, such as divorce, must happen to anyone. Is God preparing us for a life we should have chosen for ourselves but didn't? Is he acting as a parent to protect us? Or is he shaking things up because we are getting too comfortable in our own shoes? As for my friend, she is tough and mentally strong—she's had to be in survival mode for these past few years. But, at some point the tears fall hard and a box of tissues isn't enough to stop the stream of water. I prayed hard for her so that her pain would subside and that a resolution was in the works. I know that God has a plan in store for her—it's just taking a little longer than what she wants right now. I know her pain—more than she knows. It's like a death that will not go away quickly. I consider her a true friend who just needs a gigantic hug right now. God, take care of that, ok?

Just when enough time has lapsed and I really thought I had a handle on where I am today, life has a way of bringing me back to reality. Just after my ex left, I had a dream that really hit me, which I still remember to this day. The dream started in a home that my family had together. We were in a flood zone, and with the recent heavy rains, the floodwaters were rapidly coming towards us. I was packing a bag for my son. Each piece of clothing was carefully folded and put into a suitcase just for him. However, my goal wasn't to pack anything for my ex or myself, just my son. For some reason it took longer than expected and the water was closing in fast. The next thing I knew, our home was off its foundation and floating down the river. All I could do was to hold onto our son (who in the dream was a toddler) and protect him. My ex was standing a good distance from where we stood, and he didn't try to comfort us. I awoke not knowing what would happen next. My heart and mind were racing so fast that I couldn't go back to sleep.

Well, last night I had a similar dream that scared me just like the last. My son and I were living in a townhouse near a river, and just as the last dream, the floodwater was coming closer. This time they didn't come as fast. I remember going outside my home and reviewing the situation. I guess I was hopeful that the water would subside, and we would be fine. However, my better judgment made me go back inside and pack a bag for him—once again. This time, my son was a teenager, and he, too, seemed clueless about what to do. I knew it was time to leave, however, before I knew it, the house fell over to its side, and we were floating down the river. For some reason, at this point, I awoke from my stupor and kept running scenarios through my mind on what I would have done differently. I knew that I had content insurance coverage just for this occurrence, and I was smart enough to get out of harms way if I

## Attempting To Let Go

needed to do so. However, I knew I had the capability to change what happened next time, but how?

Was this dream telling me that my life was going to change drastically, once more? But this time I had control over the outcome? I don't know the answer, but what I do know is that this dream made me think more than the last one. This time I could return to the situation and make it better somehow. Now, I didn't have a husband that put me last on his list and who didn't care. Now, I have a son who was old enough that could be there for me, and me for him. We were together in this mess, and we were going to make this new life work for the both of us.

I guess divorce can follow a person for years, it's just how we deal with the circumstance that makes a difference. Perhaps we can look at it this way—the day a person stops running in place is the day they move forward. Think about it, if we're always in a hurry, we never get anywhere fast. We're only tired and worn out and perhaps disgusted with what is happening at that time. If we always look backwards and remember what got us stuck in a rut, we cannot move forward and make ourselves happy. Right?

So, what can we do to make happiness come back into our lives? The only thing that really makes sense is for us to get right with ourselves. Our religious values, our self-esteem and our physical appearance is what comes first to my mind. Think about it, if we aren't right with God, and we feel poorly about our self and our life, what's our next thought? Perhaps we think we could lose a few pounds, but if we don't, do we feel bad about ourselves once more? I just know that going back to church really seemed to make those feelings of remorse lessen for me. I'm a strong person in general, but divorce really threw me for a loop. As for the weight thing, I've been on the treadmill a few times a week for the past two years and am now working on my core muscles to flatten them. Why didn't I care about myself as much as I do now? I guess it's the fact that my self-esteem was so low. I tried my best to take care of my family—they were Number one—but I was Number 2. Well, you know what Number 2 is, right? Yes, I was the one who let myself go just to make others in my life comfortable.

I made sure my family had a good life; nonetheless, my "life" was faltering. I guess I didn't count any more, because I was trying to please everyone around me. I don't even know how I allowed myself to be manipulated for so long. Well, guess what? It's my turn to shine! My 50th birthday is just over two months, and I am really trying to get into shape. Of course, I have my chocolate daily, but I've changed a few things in my daily activities to include a better breakfast and lunch. I'm not perfect and it's taking me a long time to get back into better shape, but at least I'm making a consorted effort.

## 09.

## After the Death of Divorce

I've been told a lot that "time" heals all wounds. I just want to know what clock they're using! For, that clock seems to be different with every person. I guess we must think about life in this way. As we age, we make the decision to get married to that "love of our life," but sometimes we then get divorced, and our world changes. We are then thrust out into that big wide world that once had so many opportunities, and we tend to get a little skittish. We now have new goals, and our parents and friends are more willing to NOT push us towards that sacred thing called "marriage." They know what we've been through, and they don't want to rock the boat—for the most part, anyway. We can now think for ourselves (we hope), and we know what we want out of life, for those lessons have directed us. Well, not so fast.

Think about it, my friend Barbara put it quite nicely when she said that "If I get married again, it is my choice, not an ultimatum." Yikes! She said it all when those words came out of her mouth. But she's right. As we all age and grow from our wounds from that divorce, we get to the point where we "know" what we want now? Really? Who knows? However, we could always fall back into the same situation if we allow it. Quite honestly, I've found myself in that scenario a couple of times since my divorce. Then, when the lights came on again, I felt stuck in that relationship. Plus, it was hard leaving. I didn't want to hurt that person, but deep down, I wasn't happy. The affection I wanted and felt I deserved didn't exist, and I kept grasping for something that I knew I couldn't hold in my hands.

So, do we truly believe that our inner strength will guide us to our next relationship? Will it lead to a lasting one sparked with hope? I guess we must truly get over the last bad relationship first. I think I've said it before; when I am in a department store and I walk by any items related to a wedding, I cringe. Those shivers I feel can only be compared to watching a horror movie. I don't know what it is, but getting to the point of marrying someone all over again scares the crap out of me. But, I know the implications of not marrying or even living with someone—well, quite frankly, it's being alone. Marrying someone can provide comfort, security, and the power of growing forward together. Even living with someone has some of these qualities. So, why do I feel this way? Maybe it's the fact that I know what happened to me in my first marriage could be repeated. I have been scrutinizing everything since my divorce. I don't put up with the attitude of someone wanting to do what they want at the expense of my feelings—well, mostly.

So, should we all base our next relationship on a friendship first, for we must get to know that person thoroughly? Plus, should we feel that we're "obligated" to a person forever? If we get involved with someone, shouldn't it be easy? Shouldn't it flow like a lazy river? I mean, a 90 percent to 10 percent relationship isn't healthy for anyone! I know—I was there once. I was miserable and I knew it, but I just didn't do anything about it for years. I guess the situation was "too" comfortable for me to leave? I really think that I was too afraid of the unknown. Sounds kind of crazy when you think that I thrive on change. I guess when it's not my choice to convert; it's more difficult to get my feet out of that wet cement!

My ex finally was the one who took the first fatal step that ended our marriage. I did eventually thank him for that action, seriously! However, I just didn't like how he initiated it. Besides, why should anyone believe that they're "obligated" to a person? We shouldn't feel that we "have" to be with that person—we should feel that this person completes us. Another thing we need to keep in mind are those lessons we learned while growing up in our parents' home. Were we taught to not believe in divorce and to stay together forever no matter the situation? Or did we see loving parents who molded our thoughts? Life can really be a deal killer if we are determined to survive though a very difficult marriage. Just remember—if there is a battle that controls the relationship, remember to run the other direction! I should take my own advice, huh?

Everywhere I look, I see friends and acquaintances who are going through a divorce or who have battled that journey in their past. They have been divorced once, twice, or even three times, and have gone back for more grief. One of my friends, Jenny, whom I recently talked to is on her third divorce. She left her husband due to his adulterous affair a few months back. Then, she moved out on her own and is now trying to get him to sign the divorce papers that were served to him. With his phone calls of remorse and his promise of change, he swears that he will never do it again, and he has swears that he has changed his ways. Really? Once a person cheats, they're always a cheater—if you ask me, and given the opportunity, they'll do it again. Been there, done that one, and now I, too, have that T-shirt! In her mind, she never wants to look back. She even joined an on-line dating service! Her mind set is that she can't go back to a man who has stabbed her in the back—and for quite some time without her permission. Even though he says he misrepresented himself for several months, she cannot believe that he has truly come back down to "earth."

What is it in us that we have deep inside that keeps us from trusting again? Has that bond, between two significant others, been broken—just like Humpty Dumpty—to where it can never be put back together the same way? I know I was at that point in my life when I found out that my ex was cheating, and with someone we both knew! Maybe it was the fact that I had two rules in my life that made me make a life-altering decision. I always told myself that if a man ever cheated on me or hit me, I was gone! I never thought I would have to put that statute into effect, but I had no choice. It was the hardest decision I ever made—ever, and I hope I never have to do it again.

So, what do we do when we are put into a position to choose between our children or our love life? I have talked to a few divorcees who have told me that their children were their priority. Plus, they look back now from those times and never regret their decision. One person even told me that every time she dated a guy, they would get a job in a different state. This happened to her three times. Say what? No kidding. This really happened to her. In each instance, she was not ready to make a "move" to a different location due to her underage children. I guess sometimes it may make sense to look at your life and realize that an opportunity will never come again. But what does one include in that evaluation? Do we think we now deserve what we didn't have before, and drag our children along for the ride, just because we deserve happiness? Whatever our decision, we will have to make the best of it. If our decision doesn't pan out the way we want, the fallout will not only hit us, but it will also hit our children. Plus, it doesn't matter if our children are four years old, or 40 years old, they care about our mental health just as much as we should care about ourselves.

We all want to belong to a "unit" that goes about life enjoying time together. We travel, buy groceries, and talk about our day together. When the "couple" status is no longer around, what do we do then? Are we content to always being alone? Or do we wallow in our misery in everything we do? Then, do we get to a point where we realize that we can't do everything by ourselves like we once thought? When we ask for help from anyone, do we feel guilty because we didn't do it ourselves? From here, do we throw in the towel and put up the white flag to surrender? Or do we swallow our pride, admit our faults and proceed to find that special someone who wants to be with us forever? I guess it depends on our inner strength. It may sound strange, but I've seen it happen. A friend of mine recently went through a medical issue and didn't want his significant other to go along for the ride because he didn't want to drag her down with him. He did everything to push her away when she wanted to be there for him. It was a yearlong push-pull relationship to where she was finally through with the emotional roller coaster, and she finally left. He recently admitted that he should have let her be there for him, and going it alone was a decision he shouldn't have made. Now, he wants that special someone back to spend the rest of his life with. But it's not going to happen. It's amazing to understand why and how a person thinks when they push aside someone who wants to be there for them. Whatever their reasoning, their actions speak louder than words. Being with someone, there should be an equal exchange. So, let that person be there for you and you for them!

For the most part in this book, I've talked about people trying to get back up on their feet after a terrible relationship. Well, here's a new twist. What if your life started out with an ex-significant other, a child and chaos? You've broken up with that person you thought you wanted to be married to forever, and now you have a child to care for. Well, as fate would have it, you finally find that person you want to be with for eternally. Well, everyone around you thinks your life should start off with a wedding, a reception, and a happy life. Well, you've thought about it, and you and your significant other just want to go to the Justice of Peace and get married. However, your family thinks your plans are progressing towards a wedding date. Well, you decide that the time is right to get your marriage license, and the Justice of the

Peace has time to marry the two of you. You then decide to go for it! Well, this really did happen to the son of my friend.

Now, should everyone be mad at them forever that they were not included in their friends' ideas for a perfect wedding? I don't think so—they have a right to do what they want. They both agreed to the decision of marriage, and even though they made a snap decision to marry without the "permission" of their family, they did it for themselves. Sure, the family missed out on their special moment, but isn't the main topic their happiness? You betcha! When I heard the two of them had "ran off and got married," I laughed. It probably wasn't the most respectful comment on my part, but after I had a terrible day, I needed a little comic relief.

So, shouldn't we all jump into something we know is right? Or should we wait and let our family and friends tell us what to do? Either way, we may miss out on an opportunity, or we could be making the worst decision of our lives. Life is such a crapshoot sometimes. Perhaps we don't always know what we need to do at any moment in time, however, we must look at it from all sides and sometimes just "jump" into the deep end of the pool to test the waters. We could sink or swim, it's just the way we have prepared ourselves that will make our decisions come to light.

I guess life is like a snowstorm. It comes at you when you're not ready for it and it can last for days which could paralyze you. You can't move, and the coldness of it surrounds you like nothing else. You can't get warm no matter what you do. Scary, huh? You want so much to see the bright sunshine again, and you yearn desperately for it. The frosty feeling in the air cannot compare to what we need in our heart to heal—even after years from that dreaded day.

Divorce can also affect other areas of your life and for a very long time. If you're an emotional person, your situation is all you think about. It spills into other areas of your life, especially work, to where your boss is yelling at you for simple mistakes that you make. It can get to the point where you never really recover and now your boss thinks you're a "screw up" because you can't effectively do your job. Even though you feel that you have recovered quite nicely. It doesn't matter what things you do right, your mistakes will always take precedence. You will always be considered an employee who needs to find another job. Plus, if your boss has never gone through the same tragedy, they will never get it. No number of words can explain to them the loss you have suffered. Your wounds are healing, but you still need some time for your ex to completely disappear. Some bosses will never understand the meaning of divorce, but they will never let you forget what misery they went through while your tragedy unfolded.

Now, here's the flip side of your divorce fallout. Do you ever get your boss to recognize that you're now beyond that heartbreak? You can be productive again and she or he doesn't have to "pick" on your little mistakes. They make mistakes too, right? Since they have never been through a divorce where their "soul mate" has cheated on them or has just left them, they have no clue how it feels. It also seems that certain personalities and people in charge do not mix. If they are having a bad day, look out! But, if you are having the same, you must suck it up and go on without any feelings. You know I'm right! I've been through it and still trying to recoup.

Perhaps change is something we must put into gear in order to get to the next chapter of our lives. Some people have gotten to this point and are still struggling with any new alterations. Sometimes, however, it is quite necessary to leave an old situation behind even after years have lapsed. I guess it's time to ask God for a direction in life and where one should go next? I know I've asked for a route to my next gig! The man upstairs has heard many conversations from me lately regarding my next move. Sometimes, it takes longer than we think to regroup with our lives because we don't know where to go next. Someone please find that arrow and point to my new direction, ok?

So, when we get on that new path, aren't we sometimes reminded of times past? For example, when someone invites us to his or her wedding, don't we wish we could come up with an excuse why we can't go? Going to a wedding now makes us think about our own wedding, right? Those happy times we once had ourselves come flooding back. However, the unpleasant thoughts seem to be more prevalent than the happy ones. The happiness we once felt, the smiles placed upon our face by that event, and our first kiss as a happy couple are just now a faint memory.

As I look back at my own wedding, I remembered that my ex and I only danced once (because we had too) and at no other time in our married "career." I guess he didn't like to dance as much as I did—now I figured it out! Hello? Anyone home? Guess that door shut behind both of us, huh?

I suppose in any marriage there needs to be balance. Too far to the right or left leaves a person struggling to keep their equilibrium. Sometimes I look back and think that I had to lose my heart just so I could find it again somewhere down the road of life. I presume some people think that us "divorcees" need a new significant other in our lives. Why do they think this way? But, if this is the case, how long do we wait for that intimacy again? We never lose those same feelings of love for our own children. Then, why would we deprive ourselves of a feeling that could grace us—once more?

The road of life seems to be taking us down unpaved, rocky roads that veer in and out of tunnels and leave us afraid. For example, yesterday I found myself cleaning out some papers, and then I ran into an old cassette tape—yes, a cassette tape. How long had I had it? It was at least 10 years old with music I hadn't heard for a long time. I only held it for just a few seconds, and then I tossed it into the trash without a second thought. I didn't have a cassette player anymore, so why keep it? Perhaps this is what my ex thought about me? There was now someone new in his life, and now I didn't exist in his eyes anymore. Besides, I got smart, so he couldn't "play" me anymore either—just like that cassette tape. The relationship we had was old and was no longer desired; at least that is what it felt like to me. The "music" had faded and wanting it in our lives was also tossed aside.

I guess one way to question if we should have someone new in our life is to figure out if we can commit to another person. Both people must desire to be together as one. So, running from possibilities that could happen can take years. The balance in our lives is what can heal us—right? So, where is the medicine that we need to return to our "whole self" again? Even if we have reached that point of calm again, that screaming car can come at us from the side, where we aren't looking, and strike us. It's that off balance feeling in our personal life that can throw us off by a new love. Now we have someone else we need to juggle. But how many things can we throw up in the air at once and still remain in control? Boy, I wish I knew!

## Attempting To Let Go

Remember our teachers in life; they are all around us. We laugh with them, and we love them as we love ourselves. It's only when we finally let go of our control of our future years do we find what we want and need to fulfill our soul. Does this mean we take another chance for love? Perhaps. Well, this time we are more cautious. How about you? Does a new relationship make you think about running the other way, or do you freeze your stance? Do we also get to the point when any person who tries to take advantage of us, make us so angry we can't think straight? Then, do we allow our anger to strike so rapidly that we shield ourselves against their actions? Think hard on your future decisions, for they will change your future actions.

So, do we now put off our old ways and welcome new ones? God teaches us to live according to the Bible, but do we only make decisions according to our own thoughts and decisions? Are our tender mercies on life's events not the same as the rest of the world? Plus, will we always harbor some hatred towards those who have made our lives so miserable? Or do we just need to quit wasting our energy for such rubbish? Sounds like something we may first think at first, but when we give it a lot of consideration, what we do will ultimately define us. Our moral goodness, that I know everyone has somewhere—or not, will be our guidance to our next relationship. Because no new relationship needs that much baggage—right? I've seen some people—both men and women—take those old memories to a new relationship. Then, they mess up! You've seen it. The struggles they just left are repeated in the next relationship. Don't we have to get ourselves right before we share ourselves with someone new? Well, that's a no-brainer!

I guess one way we can look at a new relationship is to evaluate ourselves and what we want that will make us happy. We can only then lift others in the process. By this I mean, we have the power and wisdom to control what takes place in our lives—but only if we think hard about it first. Our reaction time can be quite rapid if we let it. How many times have you been on the highway and some driver cut you off? Well, in my case, my mouth usually says something my teenager shouldn't hear. Then, my adrenaline usually shoots through the roof of my car. We've all been there; it's just our reaction that teaches others what is appropriate and accepted. If we teach our children the rules, we know we shouldn't live by, what injustice have we just committed? Sometimes it's just too easy to throw in the towel; we must stay in the fight. To forgive or not to forgive those who have hurt us, can cost our soul so much. It can eat us alive if we let it. When terrible events occur, we can become miserable, but only if we allow it to happen. However, it will only occur if we can't let go of those memories that have hurt us so deeply. We must remember our past, but not let it consume us.

Nonetheless, just remember this, love keeps no record of wrongs. Besides, shouldn't we promise our kids that they will live the life that we never got to live, because they deserve it?

## 10.

## *Happily Ever After-- Whoever Came Up With That Crap*

When we think we can be happy being on our own and things have settled down, guess what, someone just changed the rules. For example, today I heard on the news that my astrological sign has changed! Say what? I was a Virgo for 49 years and now I'm a Leo—I don't think so! I even looked up what traits I am now supposed to have, and they are: Pretentious, Domineering, Melodramatic, Stubborn, and Vain. I thought being vain meant you are more likely to cheat on your spouse! Oh my, is my distention still out there? A Leo is considered very independent, but they must be in control and have a person to admire and appreciate them. I didn't realize that I turned into someone I didn't know!

## Attempting To Let Go

This article even stated that Leo's don't hold a grudge—I'm not sure that's really accurate. I admit that I hold a grudge way too long. Maybe it's the fact that I trust people from the day I meet them, but only until they give me a reason to change my mind. Then, guess what? I have a really hard time renewing that trust, or I just let that relationship go away for good and wash my hands of them. I've done it before, but only when I was involved with a friend or in a relationship that created more effort on my part than theirs. I truly believe that a 50/50 relationship is imperative for any relationship to work. I've said it before—one person cannot rely on their partner for everything. Because the scenario usually plays out that they must put in some effort at some point, and then they're unhappy! Gee, I never saw that coming! Not!

There was a part of this article on horoscopes that really made sense and made me really think. Check it out!

*"Leo has an amazing ability to bounce back from any feelings of despair or unfortunate events. They do not like to be unhappy; it hurts their pride so they will take matters into their own hands and make things right again. Leos could come into conflict with other powerhouse types of people who will not take orders and not give an inch, Leos will not budge their opinion, they will understand and accept opinions of others, but they do not take well*

*to people to try to impose their beliefs on them. Leos most often have the temperament of a demanding, spoiled child but this is only shown if someone steps on the boundaries of their kingdom. They react this way because of their territoriality."*

Gee, I guess I'm totally confused on who I've become? I thought I knew who I was, but I guess I'm now confused. But do we really know who we are now after a tragedy has "changed" us? Is the reflection in the mirror of ourselves or of our past that is now revealed? Can we still see ourselves as we once were? If we are a shadow of something else, where is our substance? More stupid questions, huh? I guess the patience and comfort we hold so dear can be the hope we need to continue in our quest to prepare ourselves for the fight.

Another way to look at life is to not be hasty in the way we live. Just think, if God were to appear in the next hour, how would we be living at this moment? Plus, if we knew what would happen in our future, how do we examine and perhaps reverse our current ways? I guess it's how we prepare ourselves to deal with the challenges we face that determines how serious we are in our ambitions. Just think, if we knew what the future would hold, we could make sure a certain part of our past is erased. But what would we learn, if anything? We sometimes cannot let go of the past because we can't forgive the actions of others and move forward. Why, you ask? Sometimes there's something there that eats at a person and doesn't let go of the grasp. You so desperately want to go forward, but something has your hands tied— we cannot forgive and move towards a future we all deserve. I know I have a hard time with that task!

I guess the best way to move forward is to prepare our hearts with a plan and then lean on God. We must take a hard look at ourselves to see if we need to get ready for a serious ambition. I guess what I mean is that we need to realize that the energy we use to be mad at our ex, can be used towards making our lives better. Our past cannot be erased, and we must understand it will always be a part of us. We have an obligation to ourselves to let go and forgive those who treaded on our heart so violently.

Then, we must realize that we may be at our lowest point—but we can only rise from here. When one gives you a ladder to get out of that hole, don't say, "No thank you." Grab a hold of the reins and start climbing upward! Being at a standstill when you have climbed that last rung of the ladder will not get you to the solid ground. But you must start placing each foot on solid ground—remember you have taken your first steps. Leave those burdens in that cold crack in the ground. My advice is to live your life not governed by a past. Leave that baggage behind. Kick it, throw it, toss it, but get it away from you. I guess its one's mature thinking that pushes us forward, for it does not kill us on the inside. The repercussions of our refusal to let go can also crush the people around us because they can also feel our pain.

I guess my words sound like the first day after a divorce, huh? It may feel that way because if we look back and it's been years since that fateful day and we have not grown, we are emotionally stuck! We have not pushed our lives forward. Guess it's like getting stuck in a hurricane. The wind and rain are pounding down making any type of movement impossible. Then, we feel like we can't make any decisions because we really are immovable.

Here's one way to look at life. All things can work together for good, for if we live with our faith and the knowledge from our past, we really can get over that "camel's hump." There are theories to the truth in life. Each time we get deeply hurt; God can use our understanding to advocate for others who have gone after you. Just think, wisdom is an understanding of knowledge. Each lesson in life we learn reveals what a trial is all about. If we keep reliving a particular trial, we obviously have not learned from it and moved onward. I've known many people who've gone down that relationship walk, and they end up finding a new significant other with the same personality as the last one. Why? Personally, I think it's comfortable and familiar for them. There's a quote in the Bible that inspired me recently on this topic—it goes something like this—if any man lacks wisdom, let him ask. Wow! Our guidance is out there and all we need to do is ask for it. What a concept!

I guess glimmers of hope bring new meaning when times are bad. If we got everything we asked for, we'd be the biggest group of spoiled brats in the world! But, if we acquire wisdom, do we live it out or toss it aside until times get tough? I've known men who have lived a certain way for years and it's only after a tragedy occurs in their lives is when they wake up—seriously! For example, a guy I dated a while back was so head strong and unyielding when it came to his feelings about relationships, until his recent medical scare. Now, he is looking back and wondering why he wasted so much time worrying and not letting people into his life who mattered. Why is it that we must learn the hard way? Do we only need our faith when we struggle, but we must go through misfortune to get the wisdom and understanding to live our or current life? Then, after the storm has passed, do we forget what promises we made to ourselves? Now, we're back to square one again! I guess we must figure out if we are walking in wisdom or walking in doubt. For, the doubt we have about relationships will eventually make us doubt God and his existence. I guess wisdom can equal stability. We can only hope.

Don't we always think too much about what we can't control? You've done it, right? Each time something happens, different people have different ways of dealing. Some are consumed, but others are cleansed like the purification of gold. Say what? Well, when gold is smelted, it is heated to the point that the pure part sinks to the bottom and the junk is swept off the top of the mixture. Isn't that the way we need to be? The junk and the pureness in our lives need to be visible so that we can distinguish between them both. We don't need all the stuff in our lives that really doesn't mean anything—right? I guess sometimes we get a little spoiled and think that we truly desire it. It's like a person who makes a lot of money at a job they hate. They like their current finances, but getting those green backs in our pocket can be mind numbing. The vehicle they drive is over priced, their home is too big for them and they have money to burn. They could even be so tight with their money that they expect everyone around them to provide their needs, but they don't reciprocate the same towards you. Seriously? I bet we've all known people like this—so why then do we still have them in our lives? Do we think that somehow, they will add to our lives in some financial way? Or is it impressive to say we have such a powerful friend? Has money become our evil pursuit? Perhaps. I guess it's like being taken out of a place of comfort, we are out of our element, and we don't know what to do next. Allowing yourself to deal with your pain from years ago is the next step to becoming happy again. Just remember, we will have trials throughout our lives—

one ends and a new one will begin, and just when we get comfortable in our current life.

I guess examinations on a life can really consume a person, but only if you let them. Do we get bored to the point of no return, and we then wander? Was this the start of that demise called divorce that we went though oh so long ago? Did we reach out for something that we couldn't have at one time, or did we reach a little farther and achieve our success? Remember, if you want something you never had before, then you must do something you never did before, to get it. Interesting concept, huh? Think of it; it is true. Life can be a little scary when you're doing something you've never done before because you don't know the consequences hold for you. I know that every time I try something new, I get a little nervous. I have learned to take a deep breath, plan, and then jump—it's hard, I know, believe me! But, when that "opportunity" window knocks, make sure its not painted over and its not stuck. Because it's hard to get it open if it's jammed shut by emotions. Remember; don't miss your chance if you know it's meant for you.

When you were a kid, was there no apprehension when you did anything? You played in the water knowing it was just wet; and there was no fear of drowning. But as you got older you realized that staying afloat was the most important thing when you were in water above your head. I guess it's just like life. Sometimes we get in a situation where we don't know what to do. We are not always prepared for what life throws our way—like death and divorce. There is no handbook, no college course and no one person who embeds, in your brain, the preparation to deal with these challenges. We can only ask for help from those who have paved the path before us. We look for answers in books from professionals who "know" how to deal, and we lean on our friends so we can vent our cries of sorrow.

If you think about life, we are part of the "animal" kingdom who can think creatively, express our words into song, and pick ourselves up after a tragedy. So, why then can we not trust each other once more? I don't know about you, but I've known people—both men and women—who have vowed to never get married ever again. Why? People have asked this question previously, but did they ever get an answer? Or is there a definitive response that has just not been found? It's like going through a major illness and then one day waking up to realize that we are alone, and we don't want to be by ourselves for the rest of our life. Besides, when do we reach this creative reasoning—it sure isn't when we are in our 20s!

Perhaps we must be almost retirement age before we mentally prepare ourselves that we were meant to have God in our lives and a significant other beside us in our bed. The love we have received from that man upstairs needs to be shared down here on earth. We just need to get to a point where we can trust once again. Even though our heart has been broken and perhaps more than once—and very badly—there really is a soul mate out there for us; I just know it! Some people may not agree with me, but that's ok. These individuals have taken an oath to be alone and that's good enough for their expectations. I applaud them for taking a stand; however, I also feel for them that their life cannot be shared with a special someone—even just for a small moment in time.

Recently I was sitting near two females who were having a conversation about life's issues. One lady said something that really hit home. Her comments were, "We can't complete another's journey; we can only help them along the way." After I heard this, I was stunned. Think about it; we stick by our friends and family to a certain extent—sometimes forever. We give them advice, hear their voice when they're in need of our presence, and we stick by them in their time of need. But have we really been placed in their lives to tell them what to do and how to do it? Plus, if they don't do as we say, do we get mad because they have not taken our advice? Then, do we give up on that relationship? If we are true to that association, we put up with a lot—thick and thin, right? Of course! We may not like what we hear from their lips, but we wish them well—always.

A day in the life of a person who doesn't have that special relationship can be a very lonely one. But do we have to base our life on having, once again, a person to fulfill us? I guess it depends on our inner strength. Perhaps a person wishes they had that special someone in their lives when they are sick and all alone. But other times they can be strong enough to weather the storm. It's only after the storm has passed that we can see the clouds' part and realize that a new beginning is just over the horizon. On the other hand, we sometimes need a little more attention to feel that anyone truly cares about the fact that we are on this planet. I guess the only question we should ask ourselves is will that person, that you expect to be there for you, be afraid of getting your "sickness?" You know that flu which causes you to run in the other direction of the one you were meant to be with? Or do they have the "medicine" to confront their ills so they can think clearly? Can you say, "Germafob?"

The fear of thinking we will get hurt, can and will drain the power we have in our lives. Our concurrent depression can then create severe weaknesses in our everyday life. Then, if we walk in fear, our ability to look to God for assistance will be depleted. Our failure and fear can be held so close that it cannot go away—not even by us, the owner. We can also be afraid if we veer from it and strive for a different life that brings freedom to our current life. So, what is the answer? My advice is to look deep within our souls to realize what is important and what will drive us down that "happy" road once again.

## 11.
## Help Me Understand

Life never really makes "living" easy. We often wonder why people come in and out of our lives—and then back in without warning. For example, what are we supposed to do when a "lost love" wants us back without any warning? Are we to jump at the chance to welcome them back after they faded away without our permission? Plus, how do we forgive them when they hurt us, when they caused the breakup in the first place? Why would we even give them a second chance when they have taken our heart and stomped on it repeatedly?

I guess life is so filled with questions that we cannot readily answer. Our "confusion cup" overflows to the point that we crave answers until our heart hurts. We are torn in different directions and pressured beyond what we can bear. I don't even know where I'm going sometimes, but I sure hope that I arrive soon. For, the world keeps spinning without my permission! Can I get off this merry-go-round; I'm exhausted!

I guess I'm not the only one in my position. My girlfriend, Amy, is getting back into the dating world. She, like me, at one time joined an on-line dating service. She is meeting so many men—more than I ever did and I am happy for her. Also, she is finding out that the dating world is different now. She was with her husband for eight years and since that time the dating scene has totally changed. She is finding that men from their early to late 40s have younger children. They are "broken" in their mind, and they think they want or perhaps "need" a relationship—but she's not sure that is the case. These men are bitter about their divorce, and they can't forgive anyone—especially, themselves.

I guess each man wants to get back out there, but they just like her, they have no clue how to do it. They either have a total attitude about themselves because they "walk on water and do no wrong," or they completely have no confidence since their breakup with their significant other. I guess my question is when does a person finally acquire the confidence to get back into the dating world? Do they need to get physically fit by going to the gym five days a week? Or do they go on some crazy diet to loose the weight they think that jumped under their skin during the chaos of their breakup? Whatever the reason, we sometimes do something foolish things to "fix" ourselves.

As for me, I have met men in their 50s who have the same common denominator—they don't seem to have a clue what they want although they think they know! Plus, by this time in their life, they are starting to fall apart medically, or their kids have a crisis for which they have to fix, and now they are totally consumed with everyone but you. I guess it doesn't matter what century it is or your current age, life just presents you with little gifts to irritate you, huh?

It seems life's little lessons really can get to us sometimes. If we look back at what we learned through every little test, are we a shadow of our past? Or have we grown beyond those examinations to become something greater? I know that when I look back at my past, I don't want to re-live it, but I'm glad to have experienced those moments that gave me grief. Really? Sounds a little strange, but it's true. All along that trail of moments, I reached out for that higher power, God, to help me finish each test. Do I now hear the words of others very differently? Of course I do. I guess it's like going through cancer treatment. The radiation, the chemotherapy, and just being deathly ill makes you want to be on the couch and lay around for days or even weeks. All this alone time gives you a new outlook on life. You

## Attempting To Let Go

see the world around you very differently and you cherish family and friends more than you ever had before. You appreciate what you have, and you want to correct those who you've wronged. Believe me, I've seen it. I dated a man on and off for over a year after my divorce. He was diagnosed with cancer, but he has conquered the battle. I know it wasn't easy for him. It also wasn't easy for our relationship. We both changed during that period, and we never made "us" a complete unit. We grew apart during that time all due to his fears of the future. I wanted to be with him, but he pushed me aside constantly to save me from his fears. I finally gave up on "us", but now he wants me back--AGAIN. Who pulls that kind of crap? I guess I've tried to figure out why men want to "do it all by themselves," but I guess I failed that test! When they finally figure out that they can't handle life's big and little issues by themselves, only then are they ready to reach out their hand for assistance. However, the help they were once offered may not exist anymore. The hurt feelings between the two may never heal. However, each one will always hold a piece of that relationship. But, once you give away your heart and it is stomped on for a long time, it is hard to heal. The trust has been trampled on with cleats, and the puncture wounds are quite present. We may eventually grow apart for good. But he is ready to find his soul mate; on the other hand, am I?

The strange thing about knowing him, and I've said this a couple of times, is that I still want him in my life in some way. He would be there for me in any capacity—even if just to rescue me from an incapacitated car. He is caring, loving, and overall, just a good person. With our history, however, my "trust factor" in a loving relationship has been skewed. Maybe I'm just not ready for his love; perhaps I'm not ready to get "hurt" again? At this point I don't know. Plus, I know that whenever I think about getting married again, to anyone, I cringe. Cold shivers go down my back and I have an overwhelming feeling of "I Don't Think So" once again.

I think we all want someone to make us smile, right? We long for a person to act crazy with and to share special times along the way. We want to see their softer side and be there for them when they fall. However, the constant feeling of being rejected once again is one that fully scares some people. This includes me, to the point of never realizing that that special person can fill the voids in my life. I've said before that it's very important to forgive yourself and others around you when something happens to hurt you deeply. I mean, don't we all want to love and be loved? Well, that's a no-brainer, but we really need to live without regret to heal.

One thing I have learned from this experience is that we should exhaust our past resources to make future peace. At this point, we must acknowledge our problems and ask God for help. For, if we purge to remove our sins, we can only then walk in hope for our future. Think about it, it's easy to fall "asleep" in our quest—especially with the church—and, especially, if your faith isn't a part of your life. Historical events in one's life come with continuing events. We can learn from life and not be afraid of moving on, however, we tend to get stuck with what could happen the next time. Our relationship with a new significant other can affect our psyche to the point of no return. On the flip side, that person may be thinking the same thing. So, can we win the battle? Who flippin' knows!

So, now that you've experienced several relationships since your divorce, where do you do go from here? What are your thoughts about where you want to be in the future? Have you and the next Ms. or Mr. Right gone wrong. Well, I will not have an ultimatum put on me that puts me into any category. But don't two people have to be ready for a relationship and at the same time? I still wonder about the sanctity of love and being together, for it happens when it's ready—I guess.

I have pondered on this problem for a long time, and the conclusion that finally hit me is that I wonder how two people can get married for the first time or ever again! I guess it's like having a baby. A woman is only fertile for about three days a month, however, there are so many pregnancies that "just happen." Call me confused! Divorce has really made me think differently. I don't expect things like I used to. I have gotten to the point where I think I can make it by myself. Plus, I truly believe that I will not be pressured to become married ever again—not by family nor by friends! I feel so free sometimes now. I live by myself, when my son is not with me. I can also come and go as I please. It's so different. Have I finally become an adult at the age of 49? Will things change at the age of 50? I guess I'll find out for this year, 2011, I will have lived for half a century. Yikes!

One thing that still bothers me about my divorce is the phone calls from solicitors who still think my ex currently lives in my house! I think I've gotten at least 20 phone calls in the past year and a half from banks, salesmen and credit card companies who still think I'm married to that idiot! Every call I get makes me more troubled. I usually get so ticked at them that I tell them about his torrid affair—or at least that he had one and he's still with her! I mean I've changed just about everything in my life but my home phone number! I guess that should have been changed too, huh?

His actions caused me so much grief and it's still happening. When do I get my "total" life back to where I don't have to deal with him anymore? Will it finally be changed when my son leaves the nest? Or will I still have to deal with him when my son gets his own life and has children? Well, this is what I have been told by others who have gone before me. I don't have room in my life for this kind of energy.

Plus, my son, to this day, tells me what his dad and his girlfriend do in their home. Read my lips: I DON'T CARE! My energy level is so warped at this moment, and the wind is out of my sails. I need to lay down and rest, and for a long time.

Just when you think you've moved on, someone or something always seems to drag you down once again. It's a definite downer, and it makes you very lonely. Your heart is heavy, your breathing slows, and your appetite lessens. The sadness you once felt comes back full force. It only lasts for a few minutes, I hope, because I don't want to hurt like this forever. I guess those feelings that hurt us so deeply never really go away. They're always there to peak their dirty little heads out when we don't have our hammer to put them back into their little opening. Sometimes I want a refund for the last 20 years of my life!

I've concluded that divorce is like the flu. It sneaks up on you, attacks you personally; you're not up to par for a particular time, but finally it leaves you. However, it sneaks back sometimes when you're not looking. For example, yesterday I ran into a person that my ex and I both knew. It had been several years since I saw her, and when I did know her, it was only in a professional capacity. Why now? Why was it my fate to see her once again? She didn't know of our divorce, nor did she know the specifics on why we split. She wanted "his" phone number and for some reason, and I didn't give it to her. She needed it for reasons that dealt with my ex—not me. I don't even know why I "protected" him. For once in my life, I didn't understand my actions; I was watching out for my ex's interests! Say what? I knew he didn't really care about business dealings with her, so maybe that's why I did what I did. My boss even saw the whole conversation and I was chastised. I guess she thought our words about my ex weren't appropriate around the work environment.

I think I need a new career choice. I got rid of my ex for the way he treated me, and changing careers would also rid me of anything else I want to forget. Anyway, back to this lady. She was supposed to call me for my ex's phone number last night, but she didn't. She's in sales, so I guess she's used to being a "busy body," but I don't want to be around, nor do I want to associate with anyone "related" to my ex. Maybe it's the fact that I don't like salespeople. I just can't handle that "pushiness."

This divorce of mine, that should have gone away a long time ago, seems to come back full force sometimes. I guess it's like raising children. Just when you think they've grown up and left the nest, they come back home and give you grief about why they can't be on their own. I sometimes think that I've grown past my inhibitions about my breakup, but it never seems to go away. Why can't I understand this test in my life? It makes me sick, both mentally and physically.

Memories are something we can't toss aside and even worse, they stop us from moving forward. For example, I recently went back to my old neighborhood and visited a former neighbor. It was good to see her because I value her friendship more than you know. Shouldn't we all have friends like that? I think yes. Anyway, she told me a story about the neighbor who lived behind my old house and what was happening in her life now. Well, to give you a little background on this situation, I was a friend with the couple just down the street from me. I'll call them Linda and Donald. When the new neighbors, whom I'll call Melissa and Jerry, moved in, my friendship with Linda went into File 13 (the trash can—that is). She tossed our friendship to the side like it never existed. I was really hurt. Was she really my friend at all? Or did she just want someone to talk to when she needed adult conversation—because, she did have four sons. I didn't like it, but I accepted the fact that she didn't want to have any part of my life. Maybe I was jealous—for the two of them were constantly together. I would be driving down the street and there they were jogging, and they were constantly at each other's houses having a barbeque, etc.—well, you get the picture. Then, the story had a sharp turn to the left when Melissa's husband suddenly died in 2009, then things started to change.

Ok, back to the story. I just found out that Linda and Donald have separated (over a year ago), and now Melissa is dating Donald. The ironic thing is that Melissa and Linda still live across the street from each other. Awkward! Part of me just knew this was going to happen, for a long time ago Linda and Donald had divorced when she was pregnant with her fourth child, but they reconciled and remarried. The second time lasted for around 13 years—so what happened? Was it the fact that both couples were so content while they were together, and now that Melissa's deceased husband was out of the picture; was it was time for a change? Did Melissa's depression and loneliness lure her into "his" arms because he really wasn't happy with "his wife?".

Part of me laughed at this situation, and now I totally believe in karma. The other half of me is saddened by these events. I almost feel sorry for her. Yes, this woman who tossed aside our friendship was gone forever as my friend. I almost wanted to stop by and offer my sympathy. But I didn't. Maybe it was the fact that these two women now live across the street from each other—still—and their "punishment" is evident everyday.

I guess I "knew" there was something was up when once, before I moved away, I saw Melissa getting into Donald's truck and she had a very large smile on her face. I remember thinking that perhaps he was helping her with a household chore that she didn't know how to do. Well, the other part of my brain was thinking down another path. I guess I was right!

My old neighborhood has seen a lot of tragedy. I lived there from 2001 to 2010, and I saw neighbors come and go, a handful of divorces and foreclosures, and general upheaval. I do not regret moving, because with all of the bad memories, I feel very fortunate with all of my accomplishments. I had neighbors who were wonderful and were there when we needed each other. We looked after one another but didn't interfere when it wasn't appropriate.

I know sometimes there's a lot in life to handle. With that information in mind, I guess we must know when to let go of what we can't control. When someone harms our heart, our bitterness can really affect our mood. But we really have to separate reality and what we think may happen. Part of me wanted to laugh and point my finger at Linda and say, "Karma—can you say karma?" However, I am distraught when I think another person is going through the tragedy of divorce. Am I crazy for thinking this way? I was wronged and now my compassion for her has appeared—and from nowhere. I don't understand myself sometimes.

Divorce can make us crazy, but which is worse, a happy divorce, or a happy marriage ending in death of one's partner? I've seen it now three times in a very short period. In all of these of cases, the marriages were good, and the sudden death of all three husbands has now defined their wives. I also thought it was quite interesting that all three women were initially devastated, but after a short period of time, they are still standing strong. Say what? You heard it right! So, does this say more about women and how they can be stronger than men in the same circumstance? Or am I totally off? I guess I don't know the answer to that one, but it has been interesting to watch all three women cope with the same tragedy. I applaud them all, and hope that if I am ever in their situation, I can come out of it as strong as they have. On the other hand, I've seen men get remarried in less than a year due to the death of their spouse because they can't stand to be alone! No kidding!

On another note, a recent happening in my town just made me want to grab a tissue. In my old neighborhood, a couple had been having marital issues for a while. Divorce papers were filed in addition to an abuse report. The wife and her children were still living in the home, but the husband had moved out. He must have known something was wrong, for the day before a tragic event; he called for a welfare check on the children. The day after every TV station broke the news that the wife had called 911 to say she was going to commit suicide. When asked if there were any children in the home, her reply was that they were in Heaven. OMG! I can't make this stuff up! Ouch!

It's been only two days since this happened and my heart hurts for her. This lady was only 41 years of age. What in the world was she thinking that made her feel that her only way out of a divorce was to eliminate her children and herself? Well, she survived her attempt at slitting her wrists, and now she's in jail.

My recent prayers to the man upstairs are ones that seem to have tragedy attached to them. I didn't know the family, but I know I've been at the point of no return too, but not to this level. Why didn't she seek help with friends and family? What was her mind set that made her want to "check out" of life this way? I mean, the day this happened, she was supposed to go to court about her impending divorce. What was that straw that broke her?

The circumstances that we all go through when confronted with a life-changing event can make or break us. In her case, her life has been forever changed—and not for the good. The ironic thing is that I must pass by the courthouse where she is being held when I go to work everyday. I know she is there awaiting her fate. Now, no one can truly help her.

I know that many people experience the same feelings that I have experienced when it comes to divorce. The anger, the destruction of a life, and the hurt comes back rather quickly as if it were my own. I can't get rid of it—no matter how much I try. My chest feels heavy, and I think I move a little slower. My mind gets stuck on the events, and I once again realize that tragedy is just around the corner waiting to pounce on us. It's only the way we respond to these events that ultimately defines us. Anyway, it sounds good, right?

# 12.
# Destination-"Life"

Now that we've gotten as far as we have in life, have we arrived at our destination yet? Say what? From our first steps to our first job, and then to our first relationship, we have grown and not just vertically. Sometimes it seems that we have taken a few steps backward as we have gone forward, but does it really matter? I guess, but only if we have learned from our experiences. The one thing we must remember is that God is with us always—he will never leave us unlike some people who cross our path.

Our wandering and wondering about life's little "gifts" sometimes become a challenge. Remember that passage in the Bible that states that if anyone thirsts, let him come to me and drink. Well, that statement has a lot of meaning after a major relationship has lapsed. I know that I felt all alone and scared when my marriage broke up. Suddenly, I had to do everything—and, I mean EVERYTHING, by myself. It was a challenge, but I am surviving my fight. Isn't it an issue when your routine has changed, and you have to struggle to get back into a similar pattern? Then, don't we all cringe at the thought of this kind of change? This may not be the case for some, but I know that "marriage" word makes me ill sometimes. Don't get me wrong, I haven't given up on it for the rest of my life; I just need to make sure it's right next time! Ha! What was I thinking? I'm not even sure what tomorrow will bring. I'm on my own—remember?

So, what goes on in a person's mind when they are scared to death to get involved with any significant other, once again? Have we become so stagnated in our ways that we are at the point of no return? Or have we become stale in our thinking? It's almost like breathing in, but not breathing out. Now, at this point you're probably thinking I'm crazy. But hear me out. When we "breathe" in something we really want and need, we sometimes do not "breath out" out our emotions, our thoughts, and our hopes. For now, we are alone once again, and we have forgotten that pattern.

When we are sick, we fend for ourselves. There is no one there to take care of us, to bring us chicken soup, medication, or even a tissue. If we were in the habit of someone taking care of "us" in every way, now it's different. We cannot rely on that significant other anymore. It is a very lonely time for us, for we now must become a "single parent" to ourselves. There is no one to care for us in our time of need, and no one to lean upon.

Things seem to constantly happen even months and years after a divorce that makes us realize that we are still alone. I don't know about you, but I don't like it. Till this day, we may never have our feelings in check. Our emotions are still frozen, even empty with the loss. Even when I was with my ex, I felt alone then too. He never seemed to care about my ills, since his ills were much more important. I guess with every new event, I thank him for his actions, for now I am free of that bond. Did I feel relief at the end? Maybe—but that's a really loaded question.

Sometimes we have become someone we thought we would never be in life. We don't have goals or ambitions to create a life we should have had all along. Do I have your attention now? Ok, wouldn't life be a lot easier if everything flowed like a river? If every droplet of water teamed up with another to produce something of value such as a stream, a river, or an ocean; don't we awe at their sight? Don't we marvel at the greatness of Niagara Falls and other bodies of water that are so spectacular? Well, of course we do. We wonder at the awe of nature and what it can bring into being. Perhaps we should look at life the same way and realize that there is greatness out there for us—we must find it in that haystack of life.

I guess, on the flip side, a person who is unsure about their life can be motivated to get involved in a new relationship too quickly. Or the ideals about marriage can lead us into an association that we don't want and we avoid it at all costs—even one night stands. Loneliness can really cause us to have historical amnesia. For, if we don't get out of a pattern of abuse we once had, we will repeat it. We could even get to the point, years later, where we still just want sex and nothing more. The other twist is when one of these people you become involved with wants a relationship with you, and you have turned off your emotions completely. Do we then feel that the next person's promise to a bond is phony? Now brain damage has finally set, don't you think? For now, we have become numb in every way. Any way we look at divorce, it is a new way of life and sometimes not by our choosing.

There aren't many people anymore who can say they were married until that phrase, "till death do you part" came into being. Remember that proverb? It brings back memories to me—for, they are ones I once said. So, how many people do you know that really believed in those words? Perhaps people who were married a long time, before I was born, only said those words with a passion. For today's society seems to not want that permanence in their lives. I often wonder why we have become a civilization who doesn't say what they mean, nor mean what they say. We have become complacent in our actions and thoughts, haven't we?

I have, however, been blessed to have known a couple who took their "I Do's" for real. They were neighbors of mine for four years. There were neighbors in that house before, but these two were unique. There were never any harsh words between them, and they spent time together enjoying each other's company. Of course there was the occasional raised eyebrow that made me smile. They were meant to be together, but it didn't start out that way.

I recently talked to my friend, Nadine, and she told me a very different story about their lives together. It all started more than 40 years ago. Nadine was in college and was dating another guy all together. The two of them had been a couple since high school. They just knew they were meant to be together forever. But, one day when they decided to go to the jewelry store to get that diamond, Nadine had an insight. She constantly fought with this man who wanted to marry her, but she knew she didn't want a relationship like that forever. She came home in tears, for she had based "marriage" on what she saw between her parents. These two people, whom she looked at as her idols, did something interesting, they talked to each other! Their communication technique was utilized well—for they got along as a couple—as a team.

Nadine had first emphasized that it was her high school sweetheart's engaging disposition that stole her heart. He was two years older than her, and she looked up to him. As time passed, she started to realize that he was dishonest, and her ultimate decision to break up with him was something that surprised her. She had a vision of what marriage should be—just like all little girls dreamed about. She cared deeply for him, but down deep she knew marrying him would not make for a long-lasting marriage.

Divorce was not in her vocabulary, and even though they both had a dream of what their life and career choices would be, there was something wrong with that "marriage" word. He had gone to college before her, and when she started college, things started to change. He was pursuing a law degree while she pursued a nursing career. They both had a goal in mind, but it was not marriage.

After the breakup, she was sure that he would never commit to any marriage—but years later she found out that he was still married to his wife. Just last year, she had gotten an email from him, and her husband became quite the green-eyed monster. There was no need for her husband's feelings of jealousy, for the happiness they shared together was enough for Nadine. She had no desire to pursue any other man; for, her passion was for her husband, Jeff.

Her story with Jeff began quite innocently. He was tagging along on a double date with a guy who was Nadine's date. It wasn't love at first sight, if that's what you're thinking. Her first impression of him was that he was an arrogant jerk who treated his date badly. He even approached her on another day when she was working as a server at a restaurant, and he tried to pick her up—when he had a date waiting at his table! All his egotistical actions were such a turn off; she basically told him to get lost. It seemed her actions towards him fueled a fire that he didn't realize he had in him.

He continued to pursue her romantically, and she finally relented and went to a concert with him. On their first date, they both realized that they were meant to be together. Hello, did I miss something? The long story short is that they were engaged after two months and married after six months! It goes to show you that moments in life have a way of mixing up one's feelings. No one really knows where he or she is going until a certain moment knocks on their heart.

This marriage lasted 41 years! Wow! Does that ever happen anymore? I guess time can be a confusing game when it involves another person. We could think that we know where we're going, but a catalyst comes into our life and turns us completely around to something we don't even recognize. This couple could even finish each other's sentences. Been there, done that one! But mine didn't last. Their relationship, on the other hand, involved treating each other in a kind, appreciative way.

When we look back at how our lives started with that special someone, do we ever prepare ourselves for that final moment when we are alone again? Will being scared of our future motivate us into something we don't want to do? I guess it's our family background and the people we hang out with that shows us how to pursue a person from the beginning. For Nadine, her special someone came from a background totally opposite of hers.

Our footing is challenged when our special someone leaves us because our memories can haunt us for a lifetime. We are now off balance in our personal and professional existence. Plus, no one can ever describe how it feels when he or she goes away. Both death and divorce can cause a person to relive events both good and bad. Plus, events that were once shared as a couple are now gone. But is it any different if a man dies before his wife, or the wife dying before the husband? I really think so. Years ago, when my mom had cancer, my dad was a basket case. I really believe in my heart that he wouldn't have lived much longer, if she had died first. I've seen men clam up when a major crisis occurs in their lives and their emotions are locked up for no one to see. Women, on the other hand, seem to handle their emotions better than men. We've been taught that it's ok to cry—for the most part men have been told to suck it up and go on. Sad, huh? I've said it before—that first year without them is a "trip"—and not one I want to relive.

I guess we get caught up in traditional roles for men and women, versus what really should happen in life. Society has pushed us toward a pattern of behavior that doesn't help us both personally and professionally. We work towards life's rewards and our relationship with God, but a detour in our life finds us in unfamiliar territory. We end up neglecting ourselves for we don't hear what we need to survive. We must not be stalled, for we must seek certain things in life that point to the man upstairs to get what we need—not what we want. We must get approval from God to get what we must have when we feel so low. Remember, our tears can be wiped away with his grace.

After a tragedy we are presented with a feeling of loss. Thinking soberly of oneself on an even keel will help us restore our health. However, we need a well-balanced perspective towards our new life. We must lean on that higher power to make us want to get out of bed daily. Now, new goals are in order. We must strive to go forward; however, we sometimes just need a push.

If we have lost that significant other to death, we never want to forget them. Do we display their favorite T-shirt in a frame; do we dig out their favorite music and cry when we listen to it? Perhaps little things can allow us to keep a little part of them nearby. We could even make a memory book depicting memories of the past. We have our ways of remembering them, and on the other hand, do their relatives think the same? If their immediate family was selfish, do they now want memories of your significant other? I have heard of this happening, but I don't think I would part with my happiness to replenish the hole in their heart. Then, when we walk down the street and see a couple arm in arm, does our heart hurt once more? For now, we are alone. We have been reminded that our special someone has gone away forever, or have they? Their memory is the only thing we have besides their physical belongings. However, I truly believe they will never leave us.

I recently watched an interview on TV about a couple of childhood sweethearts who were split apart by WWII. They both eventually won the heart of another; it was only after 69 years that they found each other once again. This man set out for the lady he left behind so long ago. He found her just two hours away from where he lived. They were married a year later on Valentine's Day. Just think, a couple that never gave up on filling that empty space in their hearts. If you love someone that much, it must be a wonderful feeling to finally succeed in your quest to be truly happy.

I recently realized that for a person to become happy again after a bitter separation and divorce, there is one thing we have to do. Saying goodbye to the life you shared with "that" person is the first step. We can look back and remember the happy times as well as the bad times, and they can help us learn to go forward. But, if we dwell on those memories, we are wasting our precious time. Just think of it this way, the more time we waste looking backwards will minimize the time we have to move forward. I've seen some women, as well as men, go through this trial in their lives. It's very discouraging to realize that the hurt has consumed them this much. Moving forward means that we must learn to love as God loves us. It is the faith we put into that higher power that can be productive in our lives. It is our faith that can work for us to show love and forgiveness to those who have wronged us—one or more times.

So, is our heart refreshed by our faith? Because we seem to ask why bad things happen to us when we are loyal to the man upstairs. Perhaps there is a purpose for us to become stronger even if we don't realize it now. Believe it or not, there is a plan for us. But I truly wish we knew what it was, for the not knowing is driving me to the "crazy" house! Remember God's fingerprints are all over our lives. What we do today will direct us to the next phase of our lives and only God knows where we'll eventually end up.

Our struggles sometimes, or a lot of the time, frustrate us to tears and even our friends and relatives see our pain. We just must be good to ourselves to survive. It's even hard to forgive a person who has wronged us; and, if we keep a record of these wrongs, we are wasting the paper we place those memories on. Our patient steadfastness can keep us faithful in the most horrid of times. We must be unmovable, especially from our belief system. I know it's hard; every day I deal with people who want to hurt my soul and send me to the "chopping block." I am damaged in some way where I don't know where my next step will take me. For, they want to deprive me of a relationship, a career or lifestyle I want. Why do they do this? What has made their heart so bitter with anger that they feel the desire to hurt me in some way? Are the feelings deep within their soul wounded to the point that they have never healed and now they lash out at others? Sometimes it seems this is the truth. Should I escape somehow? Would alcohol or drugs be the way for me to forget—even for just for a few hours? Or, what plan does God have for me? Should I let the rope go and completely trust in his plan? Either way it's scary; especially when you are your own means of support.

There are so many challenges that have engulfed me to the point where loneliness comes back full force. I continually feel the hurt once staged by my ex admitting to his affair. The load I bare comes back and weighs heavily on my shoulders and I have nowhere to place them. I cannot act like nothing bothers me, for it does. I can buy myself flowers to brighten up my world, but the feeling of a special someone giving me just daisies would shine like a diamond ring. Sometimes I hate my life, but I have come to reality quite suddenly when I look around at what is readily available to my eyes. The sensation of emotions I feel comes with unity and growth that has taken place with my faith. My salvation and my strength are through Him. If only it came with a hug! My tears sometimes engulf me—but why? I guess time doesn't always heal everything.

I don't know where I am going sometimes, especially today. I felt it in church this morning. With my career uncertainty and my love life still dangling from a rope, I don't know where I'm heading. The loneliness of my world still abounds. I guess it's like being surrounded by a crowd of people and still feeling quite alone. I'm not sure of other people, but when life seems to overwhelm me, I usually get a migraine—really! The stiffening of my neck muscles and the throbbing of my temple usually send me to the medicine cabinet looking for my prescription. Why do we let life or even people do this to us? The control that others have over our measly selves should be unconstitutional! I guess too many instances can have an overwhelming effect on what we do in life. Personally, I'm done with that crap!

I don't know about you, but there seems to be too many rules and regulations in a world full of stuff! We must be aware of it around us, but we can't let it make us go backwards. Remember, God brings about changes in our life to better us. We may not see it, at first, the good that will come forth, but it will reveal itself in good times. Our past, and even our future, can bond us once again—but only if we let it. Just think, we are guilty just as others, at judging people for what they do, that we won't do. We can carry the "air" of being more spiritual and better than the next person, but we may be doing this only because we want others to view us on a pedestal. Say, what? Are we only getting satisfaction for our self and leaving God out of the equation? Sometimes, I think we all get a little confused. I'm right, you know I am!

I truly believe that at one point in our lives we turn away from something that is of value to us, so that depression doesn't set in. But we have to remember that we cannot lose ourselves when we are trying to return to a "normal" life—that is, if we can figure out what "normal" is once again! Remember, we must get back that respect and love for ourselves that we once had. Think of life this way, who is the person we think about most in one 24-hour period? It's that person in the mirror when we turn the corner. Really! We get up from that alarm clock that wakes us from our sleep; we get into the shower, eat, and then get ready for the day. Of course, we think about our children and our significant other, but it is our self that takes priority in any situation. Although our family consumes our thoughts, we must care for ourselves first or we will not be able to care for them—right? Try this experiment—look at one photo of you and others—who is the first person you look at? It's you, right? Well, that's a no-brainer! Then, we usually critique our appearance. I guess somehow, we want to be in control of "us" for some reason—we want to control our fate. But sometimes circumstances seem to be out of our control, and we feel we have failed. Our emotions seem to come out rather harsh and we beat ourselves up, unlike others around us. We can be our own worst enemy—and we know it! Scary, huh?

So, when do we get to the point of desiring to do the work that God has planned for us? It seems as if we have pressure to perform in all aspects of life. Our career, our family, and our significant other all demand our time. We strive after our goals to be the "person" we have demanded of our self. Should we let what's inside of us feed us to our next point? Or does knowing what we should do make us do it? Plus, if we don't do "it," have we failed in some way? Have we let others down if we don't accomplish "those" tasks?

The way we live reflects what we believe and what we know. There are expectations in life, and if we understand what to do, but don't do it, have we failed? Do we strive to become someone that we don't even know, or do we rest in the fact that what we currently have is good enough? Boy, I wish I had life's answers, but right now, I feel all alone and without reason. One way we can understand what life has for us is to look at what we think at heart; therein lies our thoughts. They can take control and keep us captive. For, our heart can speak for us through our actions, which in turn judge us for what is done.

Try this—look at yourself in the mirror and try to forget what you look like. Then, look at reality. Do you want to lose those 20 pounds and wear a size smaller? Does a catalog show what you could look like in an outfit that is all the rave? But will those extra pounds you carry not show you in the same light? Well, that's a no-brainer! Believing and then doing is proof that you can be whom you want. It's the "starting" of your engine that can get you into "Drive." We can all bare fruit; we just need to be nourished from the inside to pursue our "fruitful" outcome.

Ok, you've come away from your mirror and reality has hit you hard. Where do you go from here? That's where a plan helps. For, if we have an idea of grandeur and not reality, it may not work. Do we think that the next relationship or marriage will work better than the last? Well, if we just jump into it, the answer is probably "no." I've known two ladies who have proven this as truth. They both met, and each married a guy within just a few months of the relationship. Both marriages have ended in divorce, and within a very short time. I guess I wonder why women, and men, "have" to be involved in a relationship after a major breakup. Does it have to do with our heart breaking into a million pieces and we don't have the dustpan to pick up each one? Were we taught that having another person in our lives is mandatory? Perhaps I will never know why people think the way they do.

## 13.

## Memories-- Happy or Otherwise

As the days, months, and now over a year has passed, I still hurt. I know that I am not alone in my thinking for I hurt more for my son than I do myself. However, my future looks better than it ever has. We may hurt for a while, but I truly believe our children hurt for much longer than we could ever imagine. They will always have the memory of "that" day when they learned their life would never be the same. Their parents would never be together again and that family unit they once knew would be gone forever. Their soul hurts so much and we feel their pain in every muscle in our body.

I know that I experience sadness for my son when he comes home and tells me about his week with his dad and "that" woman. His father and he seem to fight a lot and that makes him miserable. I know that he doesn't want to be there. But does he want to be with me when and if I date, and that person is in our home? I don't believe he likes that situation either. Will his experiences during his teenage years really affect him when he is an adult? I really believe he will have problems with relationships for a long time, especially with adults.

So, if we hurt from our past, should we get help from someone who can listen to our troubles? I truly believe so—especially for all concerned. We all need to vent our hurt so that we don't have to bear it alone. Kids need to talk to their peers and adults need to talk to their friends and co-workers. For some reason, releasing our soul to someone who cares for us tends to free our mind. The burden of life needs to go away so we can liberate ourselves from our hurt and pain.

It's a part of life when our children hurt—both physically and mentally. As parents we want to prevent things from ever happening to them. We try to protect them, but there are times we can't. We feel helpless but all we can do is hope for a better life for them in the future. We want them to succeed, to fall in love with that right person they will live forever with, and to become successful in life. I can only hope, for my son, that my wishes will come true.

What part of our life would we change if we could? In addition, what part of our child's life do we wish were different? Right now, I can think of a lot of things that I would change—my educational path and avoiding certain relationships—just to name two. I guess if we had that special Jeanie in a bottle for three wishes, our minds would run wild, huh? However, all the wishes in the world will not turn back time for we make decisions and will always have to live with the consequences. The people we meet, and the certain situations we allow our head to get us into, can take us to places we never imagined. If we could only get our heart and our head in sync so they work properly together—that would be a miracle, huh?

If we could only go back and reclaim that relationship that we know would have worked or get that perfect job and make a lot of money. Would we then be happy with life? I guess it depends on what makes a person content. If we only had fresh flowers in every room, or a 75-inch TV in every space—what is our priority in life? Is it throwing yourself into work every minute of the day and ignoring your significant other? The people we affect in our life seem to have an influence on us personally—but sometimes we don't see it until it is too late. We have drawn closer to money and not to God. Our values have changed. Plus, sometimes our goals involve everything but a higher power, which can cause us to spiral out of control.

Look at some of the celebrities out there now. They have lots of money, big mansions, and the ability to have everything they want. But are they getting what they need? Probably not. Then, they are like a corkscrew removing the cork from a bottle of champagne. The contents spew everywhere, or it makes a noise and blows up. Sound familiar? Life can also be compared to alcohol and drugs. It comes and goes, creates chaos in very respect, or it can be consumed lightly and evenly. Plus, think of it another way. If you find a person you thought you wanted in your life but they, for some reason, try to distance themselves from you, what do you do next? Do they have a "Jeckle and Hide" personality, or are they just a loner? Do they want you around only when it's convenient for you? Plus, do they only want you now because you are with another person? Their actions can speak louder than words sometimes and trying to figure out what they really want is out there somewhere. I've experienced these emotions in relationships, and I'm sure others have too. So, what are we supposed to do now? There's another question to kiss up to God!

We could even compare this situation with the people in our family. Why do our siblings, aunts, uncles, friends, etc., act as they do sometimes? They are destructive to themselves and their relationships with others. They see no problem drinking too much which causes their outrageous behavior. It's almost as if they play by a different set of rules than the rest of us. Do they really know what they want out of life? Personally, I really think they do! However, life's events keep getting in the way of reality and clear thinking. We could all stand back and watch their rants, and try to intervene, but if they don't take any advice, they are destined to fail—right? Well, maybe. Now, back to those celebrities. With all their wealth, they have too much time on their hands, and enough people to "pay off" to think the way they want them too. Then, they usually get themselves so deep into trouble; they're either in jail or six feet under. Ouch!

Right now, we have the "information" we need from our past memories, but where do we take it? In addition, once we realize that we have it, do we then live it out? Do we feel the need to put in effect a positive action plan that involves God? If we look at others and observe their actions, we may realize what is really going on out there. People are finding, craving, and seeking after things they think they want, but in reality, they sometimes have no clue what is good for them. I'm right, aren't I? What we value in life really should really be assessed. Should we marinate in what feels good on this earth, or should we realize that there is something out there better for us? Plus, where is our drive to keep going sometimes?

If we look at the past and ponder over those events, can we realize what part of our life is "messed up?" Well, first we must figure out what is in disorder, and then we can make a plan to move on, right? Well, some people make their mistakes, blame others who were in their life at the time and never realize that they played a part in it too. So, when our kids grow up and make the same mistakes, how do we judge them? Do we lock them out of the house because we are embarrassed about what they did—even though we did the same thing? Or have we shoved aside what we did, and judge others as they once judged us? There's that double standard again!

I guess life starts with God's vision for us. Because what area do we need to realize is not right in our life? What we treasure in our life, we will also find our heart. Think about it. If we treasure what money will buy us, all we will think about is how to make it—legally or illegally. It will consume us from the inside out and could take over our being. The "stuff" of the world will be our obsession. Whether or not we believe it, things happen at their own pace and we, sometimes, cannot control them. That's a no-brainer, huh? Besides, we can say and do things in a certain time frame, but then blame others when they don't work out.

Now that we've got to a point in our lives where we think we've got a handle on life, have we really managed one important part—our thoughts? Remember, what's in our heart is also present in our mind. Then, if our mind takes control, our heart usually follows. This kind of thinking can get us into trouble—but only if we let it. If we only want sex out of a relationship, that's what we'll get. If one puts their whole heart and soul into what, you and a special person want, you may be happy forever. However, there is no guarantee.

So, what does a person do with their current thoughts and memories in that gray mass? Well, is there any guarantee your past and your future will determine what you will become? Sometimes we will never know until it happens. These thoughts can change how we live our current life, and it can bring our thoughts into captivity—remember, our brain controls our actions. Our brain can make a blueprint on how we live—but only if we allow it.

Memories can be funny. They can consist of vacations, family, friends, or things we did in childhood. But what happens when memories haunt us when we become adults? Do we look back and resent certain people or even ourselves because we could have prevented those events that changed our life? Or do we look at the events happening now and wish that somehow, we could change something that has affected us so dramatically? Perhaps. Between natural disasters and life events, in general, we may feel lost. We hurt, we cry, and then we get over it—well, sometimes. We may even take events with us to our grave. Or we may never rise above those events that have hurt us so greatly. So, what do we do about them? All I know is that we cannot let those events break us. We must rise above them somehow. As we get up each day, we must find a reason to go on. Whether we use, as an excuse, our children, our parents, or our friends, we can't let devastation break us.

Speaking of memories, when we look back at the many personal relationships we have had, what is the first thing we think of? Was it the sex, the feeling you had in your stomach each time you saw them that set you afire, or something entirely different? Or did the relationship fizzle just after a few days, a month, a year, or even longer? If it died too quickly, what happened? Has anyone ever looked back and really evaluated why it expired as it did? It could have been that you spent every waking hour together and got bored of each other. Or, if it did work out for a long time, what was the glue that held your relationship together? Things that make us go "humm." They can make us happy, or they can tear us apart more than once.

Now, let's say you've "really" moved on with your life, but there are some haunting thoughts still lurking in the back of your mind. Well, here's what I mean. You find a new relationship, you get way too comfortable, but he or she does something the same way your ex did! Ouch!! What kinds of memories come flooding back to the forefront of your mind? Are you immediately upset? Or are you so furious that you tell that person to take a hike off a short pier? Do you confront them? I've had that experience lately. At first, I wasn't sure exactly how to confront him, but I finally told myself that I deserved better, and whatever his reaction, I would deal with it. When I finally got up the nerve and spoke to him, it wasn't as bad as I thought. I got the reaction that I was right in my thinking. He was very understanding on why I felt the way I did. For, he would tell me that he was going to do something, but he would go home and fall asleep. Hello? If I expect something to happen because someone tells me it will happen, and that person continues to falter in their actions, it's not fair to me. Right? Well, of course, silly! It's not fair to anyone if you look at it. Why should one person have diarrhea of the mouth and say they are constantly going to do something, but don't? That's what my ex consistently did to me. Then, he failed to be with me at all—in anything or any activity! I'm not going down that path again—EVER! No one should have to!!

Recently I heard someone say that a woman alone is a woman without a prayer! Say what? Didn't the sexual revolution teach us anything? The memories of those days obviously aren't getting into the ears of today's youth—well, that's my opinion anyway. Has our strength lessened since the 60s or 70s, or am I thinking too much? For, the world's memories should have taught us something, right? Now, if I put this in the way I feel about my ex, there isn't enough sex in the world to want my ex back!

Our memories should teach us something. What went on with our past relationship(s) and marriage(s); especially, if there was an affair involved, is a grand lesson. If these actions went on behind our backs, and then "that" person just stepped out of our lives, where are we now? Have we been just tossed aside by them without our permission? Well, that's a gigantic, YES! Those hurtful emotions that pierced our hearts so deeply run throughout our soul and right down to our toes. Scary, huh?

## 14.

## *Can I Order Another Round?*

It's hard to forget those horrid feelings, forgive our ex, and then move on. It's not like buying another drink to replace the one you just spilt. That relationship is gone forever, and it's very unlikely you will get it back—no matter how much your desire succumbs you. I can't stress this enough. It's been almost two years since I busted my ex, and I still can't deal with all of "those" feelings he put me through. I can put them in a closet and shut the door, but they always seem to find the doorknob and crawl right back to me.

I am still sensitive to situations that come up in the new relationships I've had since. Doesn't he understand what he put me through? I don't think so. I even looked up "narcissism" in the dictionary this weekend, and I could have sworn his picture was beside the definition. How do people get so stuck on themselves to the point where they don't want to take care of their partner? Was it their childhood or their parents who made promises of hope and success that never happened? Did their expectations get dashed to the point where they felt they would never succeed, so they put themselves so high upon a pedestal that now they must put all of the emphasis of the world upon their shoulders? It seems that way. My childhood had dashed dreams too, but I was never that callus about a relationship. Maybe it's the fact that I take other people's feelings into consideration before my own. Sometimes that gets me into trouble, but that's just the way I operate.

I guess you can just call me a pin cushion, because I take all that life gives. I hurt from pain, am happy when it goes away but then I "bleed." With some help, the bleeding stops—but sometimes it still trickles down and I don't see it. I take life for what it gives me. Sometimes, I let people run over me—still—and I don't know what to do about it. I want to scream, run and hide, and then disappear. What is it about my personality that shows such a flaw? Or is it really a flaw to have real emotions?

I'm not sure about anyone else, but I have made it my mission to change everything about my life since I got divorced. Am I crazy? I think not. After my ex left, I started getting new furniture. Of course, I would have never been allowed to do this before, with him—

thus, there is my reasoning, my rebellion. Then, I got a new vehicle followed by a new townhouse. I've even gotten to the point where I'm replacing the towels in my bathroom! Yikes! I don't know what it is, but I must "replace" my old life with a new one. I even want to find a new job. I guess everything that I once had, reminds me of "him."

Am I trying to prove something? Perhaps. But I can tell that everything that I'm doing is really helping my psyche. I feel better about myself, and my self-esteem seems to be returning. I'm not sure where it went, but it's finding its way back to me. So, how long this feeling will last? I don't' know. Am I returning to "normal" now? At this point, I don't realize what "normal" even means! I just know that I'm proud of myself since I have achieved more in the last 18 months than I had before I was married. That's scary, huh?

With all the accomplishments I've have seen in my "new" life, I still am seeking a goal to fulfill me. There always seems to be something going on that challenges me and most of the time it seems overwhelming. Maybe it's the fact that I'm going through it by myself. I know I've said these words before, but it's true. Shouldn't we all get to the point where we don't rely on anyone for help? I think not. No matter how strong we think we are, there is a little wiggle room for someone to go down that path with us, we just must remember that fact.

With all the challenges we are given when we get divorced, the one thing that seems to haunt us is the personal changes we go through. I know this for a fact because I now look at my ex and I see a dramatic difference. I saw him yesterday and I was amazed at his appearance. His hair is getting grayer—more than normal. His dress was a "shabby sheek" for his Dockers were frayed and tattered, and his overall demeanor seemed sad. I wondered what was going on in his head. I almost felt sorry for him—well, almost. The life he has chosen is one in which I am not welcomed. I am not there to pick up the pieces he doesn't want to place in life's puzzle. It makes me wonder if "she" is taking me care of him like I did. Does she bend over backwards to accommodate him? I doubt it. Perhaps I did too much for him, and then he decided that I should always do "it" for him.

Now that his life has taken a new direction, where will he be in a few years? I mean, it's been less than two years since my fateful decision to "bust" them both. They, not I, chose to cancel our "so-called" marriage. I'm just moving forward now like I've not done before.

On another note, remember Mary? Well, she's doing ok. She's reconnected with a guy she knew in high school, and they have been corresponding a lot. She's revamping her personal standards and wanting to improve herself—in a lot of ways. All I can say is, "You Go Girl!" My other girlfriend, Jackie, bought a townhouse just down from me in the same complex. Good news! I have surrounded myself with winners of all kinds. I have just lessened my load of losers by letting them go their own way—if you know what I mean!

I guess God really does have a plan for us; it's just the way we perceive it, and then we take the bull by the horns to move forward to promote ourselves. That second, third, or whatever round we receive in life, to make our lives better, always shows up, but we must recognize it and run with that plan. If you're reading this book, and you have gone through what I went through, guess what? There is a greater plan for both of us! You may think I'm smoking something illegal, but I'm not. I write from my heart when it comes to my divorce. I was not happy with my marriage, and when I found out that my ex was cheating, I knew it was over. A new life was awaiting me, but I didn't know it at that time.

It's amazing that I've talked to so many women who have been in my shoes, and for the most part they are so happy that their ex is gone! I guess they have felt the same emotions that I felt, and now that their ex is no longer in the picture, there is a sense of relief. When the initial saga has subsided, it's amazing how lives are turned around. Sounds strange, but it's true.

I guess I'm talking mostly about women when I say that when our inner strength takes hold, we run—

not walk—to the nearest exit. When we have been told over and over how worthless we are, our release date from our prison hold allows us to be free. We can smell the roses whose scent was once lost, and we can relax from those migraine headaches that once consumed us. There is a new life awaiting us; our eyes are now open to see it. God gives us life—and abundantly. We need to realize where his "test" will lead us next.

So, admit it, do you look back at your past life and smile. Or do you think that you could have done something to "fix" that itch that your ex had to make him or her leave? At this point, are you beating yourself up, or are your friends patting you on your back for your accomplishments thus far? I think my friends are doing the latter for me. The only thing that still haunts me is that my son still thinks he must tell his father everything I do. Does he really think that his father can influence me or tell me NOT to do something? Well, there's another big fat No! That man has no power over me anymore and it's quite liberating since I've arrived at this point in my life. However, being liberated does have its downfalls. I still get nervous when it comes to money and where I'll be tomorrow, the day after, and at retirement.

Sometimes I even think I should get everything I want before I get "tied down" again. I don't want to ask permission to buy anything from underwear to a new car. On the other hand, I have to be financially responsible for all that I do. I guess there's a fine line between being alone and being with someone. I just must figure out what I want. The next person I say "I Do" to, has to be on my playing field, together, with me. That "give and take thing" has to be present at all times—not just when a significant other wants it in attendance.

I feel that I have grown so much in almost two years after the severance from my marriage. I guess it's like getting out of the military—if you had to say, "Yes, Sir," and "Yes, Ma'am," so often that it made you ill, when you get discharged, you're at a "done" point. Believe me, I've done both, but the respect that I learned for people and situations is still inside of me. I had respect for people before, so it wasn't such a culture shock when I went to boot camp. However, some people weren't meant for that type of restraint. I've met both men and women who have a desire to be in charge and they have never been in the military. Personally, I don't think that they'd make it passed the first day after a Company Commander yelled at their face. People aren't like *Private Benjamin* and life isn't a resort. If you don't know whom I'm talking about, research the movie—its quite eye opening.

Now that I've brought up boot camp, I wanted to share an experience I had on my first night. After the first day was done, and we were headed to bed, I found out the next day that one lady went AWOL, and another one slit her wrists. The crying throughout the barracks was very evident for several hours after the lights were turned out. Were these women sorry for what they now signed up for? Well, it was pretty evident! Also, after several weeks had lapsed, I saw only the strong survive the test. It's just like life in general. If you're strong, you can make it over that next hill. If you're weak, people will run all over you and make your life miserable. A job is a little different. You can change jobs—but only with a plan and a lot of effort. So, where is your priority in life now? Have you planned to have another drink to escape, or is your plan in writing? I hope it's in writing!

You deserve a better life, and if you're reading these words, you have thought this at one point or another. Or, you know someone who's been there, and you may want to help him or her through their grief. Think of life this way. You now have been given another opportunity to get "it" right this time—whatever "it" is in your current life. Do you want to change something that was never quite right in your personal life? Do you think you deserve a new job and now you can push yourself towards what you deserve? Because, before your divorce, your ex always put you down and your self-esteem was non-existent. This made you not think highly enough of yourself to go for it. Well, guess what? Life has a way of correcting wrongs. It's almost like a healing pattern that has engulfed you—something you've always needed, but didn't have the medicine to mend your pain. Well, welcome to Healing 101!

Now that you've "healed," where do you go next? Say what? Do you feel you're crazy or another person saying those words is crazy? Or have we seen a side of "love" we never want to experience again? Relationships are never perfect, but we could probably find one that is close if we look hard enough. Plus, as we look back on 'those" days, did we really live half a life, for all that time? I guess the answer is in the eye of the beholder, huh?

As an example, one of my friends who got divorced last year has come a long way. Her ex was involved in drugs, couldn't keep a job, and gave her and her kids so much grief; I was surprised she kept it together. Now I hear that she has met someone new, lost a lot of weight, and is so happy. The clouds have now parted and the sun shines brightly. I'm happy for her; she didn't deserve the heartache that her ex handed her on a rusty plate.

There are so many things that we must deal with before, during, and after our divorce. I just know that I have been trying to avoid that "other woman," but my time is coming. My son is going to high school next year and his 8$^{th}$ grade graduation is coming up. My ex informed me that "she" wants to come too. Get a rusty razor blade or get a rope—that might be a little easier to deal with than being in the same room with her. It's been almost two years since we split, but each new situation still gives me chills. I've also wondered when we would be in the same space at the same time on this earth—now it's coming. At least I have a heads up about the time and place. Does she wonder what I will say to her? Or will she be more uncomfortable than me just because of our history together? Either way, it will be the longest night of my life. I think I'd rather sit on a rusty nail than be in the same room with her.

I guess part of me wants to thank her for taking my used luggage from me and recycling it for herself. The other part of me sees her as a cheating, manipulative, and conniving woman who will do anything to get what she wants. I mean she did the same to her first husband. Perhaps that's why I haven't talked to her at all during the past, almost 24 months. I have enough drama in my life—I don't feel like I need to create anymore for myself now. However, I truly appreciate what I now have in my life, and since I have put my religion back at the top; there is a calm in my days and hours since my revival.

I now know that I don't have to have a relationship in my life that is permanent. It sounds strange, but I guess my freedom is very important to me. I felt so strangled for so many years, and that ball and chain followed me everywhere I went. I know some people must have a significant other in their lives; others do not need the grief (as they tell me) to destroy their personal style. It's nice to have someone beside you, don't get me wrong. I guess it should be the right person, and everything should click. Just like a seat belt, it must hold you in place, make you feel secure, and then keep you safe in your journey. It's all in what you want to make you happy. Shouldn't that be our goal?

## 15.

## *I have the aspirin, where's my headache?*

With everything that happens, when our new as well as old relationships sour, what is left are the pieces that our children are forced to pick up. I know that my son is still struggling with daily tasks, homework and living in two locations. With all the changes now, the only two things in his life that seem to be unchanged are being with his grandma and attending karate classes. These two things are, what I think, keeps what little sanity there is left in his life. I just know that his bursts of frustration, get my juices going and I need a stiff drink. Guess that old saying is true, "What is God's revenge for having sex? Teenagers!" Just add a divorce and see the explosion occur quicker.

The next thing in store for my son is changing schools in the fall. He will be attending a very large high school, and I don't know how he will deal with another "change." He is so dead set on keeping his life frozen in time. Doesn't he know that life is full of changes, and we have to deal with them as they get thrown our way? Sometimes I don't have any answers to anything. Gee, I'm the parent of a 15-year-old—what was I thinking? I don't know anything! I'm just the "mom."

Now that I've figured out that I'm a parent without a plan, so where do I go from here? Everything that my ex and I do, besides throwing money at the situation, seems to be faltering when it comes to our son. His grades keep going up and down, and even though we threaten to come to his school and sit beside him in every class, he pushes his attitude on us every day. Yikes! Parenting 101 is a class I skipped obviously—at least I think it was that class.

I've gotten to the point that I wonder when my "expiration" date occurs when it comes to parenting. Now that I think about it, I don't think I have one. I keep praying so I can guide my son on life's issues, but the frustration seems more prevalent than the answers. I do have faith, however, that I will survive his "road of confusion."

Speaking of being confused. Recently, a Mega Millions jackpot reached over $300 million. A group of co-workers in New York threw their money into a pile and bought some lottery tickets. As one of the guys stopped by a convenience store and got in line to pay, he reached down to get a candy bar. Suddenly, another guy cut in line in front of him. Instead of him saying something to the guy about his rudeness, he just let it go. This rude guy bought a ticket ahead of him, and when this other guy got to the counter, he also bought some tickets. After being interviewed about this event, the gentleman who bought the winning tickets said that this guy's actions allowed him and his co-workers to win.

Think about it, eventually it's our actions that allow us to succeed or to fail. We could see life as a challenge and then just roll with the punches. Or, we could complain, kick, scream and blame others because what happened to us is "their" fault and not ours. Remember, life does not ask our permission in the good times nor in the bad. We are left to fend for ourselves—but God is always there so we can ask for that direction. He will answer, but it may take time. I know I don't have much patience when it comes to waiting; it's been such a challenge for me.

I've asked for the right direction many times in my next move, from the man upstairs, but the answers come slowly Waiting seems to be the hardest. I guess I just want things to happen too quickly. The word "change" is very comfortable in my vocabulary, and I welcome its presence. My son, on the other hand, "freaks out" at the very notion of the word "change." I guess I don't understand why he sees the world as an environment that does not modify itself—in any respect! Why? Is someone's world that fragile that they feel any type of change is unwelcome? Or do they have a fear of the unknown that scares them because they are so near the edge of the cliff, and they are ready to fall off?

I've often wondered why people can't accept challenges and journeys that take them outside their comfort zone. Maybe it's the fact that I was the youngest child, and I didn't like my surroundings. I wanted things to be different than what they were, for what I was handed was what I didn't desire. I even remember when I was three years old and my dad was holding my brother, and I wanted to be held too. In the background, after my dad picked me up, my mother stated that carrying two children was too heavy for him. My brother got more "dad time" than me. Call me a feminist at an early age, but for some reason I remembered that incident, and I didn't like it.

Now, at this point in our lives, how do we feel about what we've experienced and where we are now? Do we think we've failed, if our "life" has gone down the wrong path? I still see people who think the opposite. Usually, these people are optimistic, happy, and full of hope. It's also interesting to view the groups of people who are totally opposite. Think about life this way, if married couples were open about their problems, both good and bad, would they ever get divorced? Is sharing all times—not just a good, a remedy for success?

I know I have gotten very frustrated with the men that I have dated since I got back into that dating game. I've noticed that when they have crises, they run the opposite way and not to me for support. Is it the fact that they are prior military and taught to be "tough?" Or is it the fact that they are men and that's what they are expected to do—suck it up and go on? In either case I have concluded that they are running scared and putting their head in the sand until the predicament passes. So, who am I to judge them? I'm just the opposite. I have a grand case of "diarrhea of the mouth," and everyone knows my calamity! Which is worse? I don't know at this time of my life, but I truly think it's the way we were raised. From the time we can walk, talk, and think on our own, the forces of life have molded us and surround our very being. How we deal with what life tosses our way is how we will eventually be as adults. Yikes! Time for that stiff drink!

Now I'm going out on a limb, but I'm guessing that each person's actions will eventually be found out—whether they are good or bad. Afterwards, do we repent our "crimes," or we just hide. In either case we may be humiliated with the results. Living a life that we know isn't right and wanting it to change is a decision we must make. So, do we just look the other way and pretend we're sorry? I've known people in my life who say they're sorry, but their words and their tone of voice are not remorseful. They throw out words to discredit others and not themselves. They do not look deep inside their conscious and make excuses for their actions, for in their eyes they are justified. Boy, where is that aspirin bottle! I sure could use it right now, because I can't figure out life!

So, you've been divorced for, say, a couple of years. You used to be bored and overwhelmed with feelings of loss. But now your time is precious. You are so busy that you can't even think straight. What happened? It seems like every minute of every day is accounted for with "whatever" project that needs to be done. You don't have any time to spend relaxing, nor to eat correctly. Everyone around you needs assistance, but you seem to be the last on the list—once more! Say what? Here again, you are the lowest priority in your life. I guess it's true that history does repeat itself. Plus, if you're not taking care of you, do you really think you can take on a relationship? Or do you feel you're just getting old, and some things are just not worth the effort. This may be true in my case.

I guess when we say, "I Do," it seems like our marriage will last forever. Our lives were brought together with those two little words. But, years later, one little word can tear us apart—"divorce." Now that we're older, have we learned anything about life? Perhaps we have, but perhaps not. We now see the world with wrinkles around our eyes and the wisdom we wish we had in our younger years. It makes us wonder, or at least me, if I knew now what I knew back then, would it have made a difference in my decision-making? I know I've said these words before, but they're always in the back of my mind.

The things that happen in a person's life when they are young seem to stay with us for a very long time. Our values, our goals, and our life's wishes all go into our marriage, but only if we take them with us. Whether or not one spouse cheats on the other, because of "whatever" reason, is the ultimate quest we must deal with it if it ever happens. It is a series of events such as: Were we too young when we tied the knot? Did we get married for the wrong reason? Or did we have a moment of "stupidity" that caused us to say those words and to sign that paper? Whatever the reason, now our age seems to be in the way of a relationship. I know what you're thinking. You believe that we can find a relationship no matter what our age! Well, my grandmother is the ultimate proof of that one. She has been married three times, and she's now well into her 80s. You go Grandma! What I am talking about is the fact that some people have said to me that they are too comfortable where they are in life now. Most of these people are in their 50s and beyond. I think our mind plays tricks on us sometimes to make us believe in a certain way. Whether or not a person thinks they are ok by themselves is a value they hold near and dear to their hearts. Remember, when you're not looking for a relationship? Well, it's usually the time when you find one!

# 16.
## A Man's Opinion

I recently had the opportunity to talk to a male friend of mine who told me about his divorce. I've known him for over a year now, and I was surprised about what he said. He's not the typical "manly man" who doesn't care about the people around him. He actually does housework and doesn't complain that he needs to pick up after himself. Imagine that? He, along with several other people I have talked with, told me that they got married too young. He had been married for around 19 years and he, yes he, was the one who cheated.

I'm not sure where his story went so wrong, but he and his ex-wife parted ways. Was his infidelity the only reason that started this story? I don't believe so. From what he told me, the relationship between them started going south when the chemistry between them behind closed doors was like ice. This is so familiar to me; for I understand that when you don't want to touch your significant other, just pass me the divorce papers and just get over it!

I guess we start a relationship by clinging to each other so tight we don't want to let go. We can't stand to be without each other, and sometimes something goes awry, and we start hating each other. The thought of that person "touching" us, in any way, is repulsive. Thus, we want a special someone to hold us and take away the pain of rejection. Right? Well, that's what my ex thinks—in my opinion, anyway. I really believe he thinks that I "rejected" him in some way, and he had to find someone to take away his ache. However, I truly believe we had had enough of each other and the thought of sleeping in the same bed was now nauseating. So, he had to find someone whom he felt was on his side. Believe me, I didn't think about cheating on him, but I did daydream what life would be like if we weren't married to each other. Ouch! There, I said my opinion, and now I've admitted my guilt. I guess my ex and I really should have talked more about what was important, but we didn't. The communication between us faltered, just like our love for each other.

What does a couple have to figure out when they meet, date, and then eventually say those, "I Do's?" I know of a couple now who are supposed to get married in just a few months and he's getting cold feet. She's 20 and he's 25, what? I think they're just too young to make such a "grown up" decision. But here's a little history. They got engaged, broke up just a few months afterwards, got back together, and now he's not sure he wants to get married. Just yesterday, he said he's sorry and he's not sure why he said those words. I've seen it before when a couple gets married too young, when they should be sowing their "wild oats." I even know a lady who's been married three times thus far, and she's only 38 years of age. Her "wild oats" are only now coming out.

Is she wrong for acting fanatical now? Maybe. But I truly believe we all go through those emotions of wanting to have fun once we have left our parent's nest. Sometimes we go too far and make decisions that will follow us forever. Other times those decisions are the best ones we've ever made. Then, we can look back and smile, or can we? We can tell those people who warned us of those "bad" decisions, they thought we were making, it was the best thing we ever did. I guess it depends on how we look at our current life that will define our goals and ambitions.

Now that we've gotten to a point of no return, where do we go from here? Do we blame that "man," or that "woman" who destroyed what we once had? Or is it wiser to look back and understand why we or they, did what they did? I don't mean that we should forgive them totally for the destruction "they" caused. It's just the fact that, in their eyes, they were correct in their actions. Really? Well, that's what they think anyway.

In this book I have noted stories from both men and women and have they have intrigued me. In every case, it wasn't just the man or the woman who had extra-marital affairs—both were guilty. Some had alcoholic spouses, and they left not for an affair, but to escape that life. Others got divorced because their maturity level wasn't there and "trying" wasn't in their vocabulary. However men or women think, we can all be uneasy with the decisions we ultimately make.

Too many games and giving up too effortlessly seems to be the easy way out when we feel trapped. Easy enough—right? Is it the fact that we get bored if all our attention isn't focused on that special person? Do our minds wonder if the distance between us is far and long? Ask anyone in the military, and they'll tell you that distance does not make the heart grow fonder—at least for some. For others, the destination to a happy marriage does not equal an affair—it equals dedication.

It's amazing how both sexes think the way they do, and when it comes to a breakup, there are usually years of going down a wrong path. I recently interviewed a man who had two former spouses cheat on him. I turned the tables and asked him why any man would cheat on a woman. I got some amazing answers. He told me that men initially see a woman for their physical appearance, then they go to their intellect, and lastly how they can carry themselves. He also said that sometimes men have a narrow view of what they expect, for they want the woman to always be this way. For example, if a woman is self-sufficient, can handle all her affairs (such as her finances, looks, etc.) a man always wants her to never change.

Sometimes either person may get too comfortable in a relationship and let himself or herself go downhill in one way or another for varying reasons. I guess getting too comfortable in a relationship can redirect a person's thinking and those former expectations can be altered. The original attraction is gone, and all we're left with is a fat, lazy slob whom we don't recognize, right? On the opposite side, one reason for a woman to stray from the relationship is if she isn't satisfied with her current situation. It could be the complacency of the relationship where her partner is taking advantage that she's a woman. This could mean many things, such as, she does everything around the house while her partner watches sports from the comfort of his favorite TV and worn out chair. Could she now see what she saw then, but with new lenses? These events could happen to either person in the relationship and make it go awry. In either case, both people could go out looking to satisfy what they think is missing.

The last reason involves a lack of communication in the relationship that creates altercations when they don't even exist.

I can agree with this reasoning and how a man can feel. I've also realized, from talking to other men, that the older they get, they too want to be taken care of—both physically and emotionally. They appreciate a woman who loves to cook, wants to work out, and be independent if need be. They want to take care of you, but they don't want to be a parent and correct you. However, there are some men out there looking for a "mother figure" because their mother always took care of them. This can be true in different cultures. Say what?

Now with this information in mind, it is totally an injustice for a parent to teach their sons and daughters to be dependant on a partner. Think about it; who wants to be with a person who is lazy and cannot pick up after himself or herself, can't keep a job, and/or criticizes you for everything you do because you're not perfect? Not me, but I feel I've been caught in several relationships like this and just didn't know how to get out. I was miserable for a long time, and even though I feel I am a "self-made" woman, I guess I was being too nice. Hello, is anyone home, because the lights are off?

We all want to feel important and wanted, but at what price will we go to get it? Our friends and family can talk to us until they're blue in the face,

## Attempting To Let Go

but we will only listen when life gets tremendously uncomfortable for us—right? I guess thinking long and hard on a decision is the first thing we should do—huh?

At this point in one's life we still have to do things—after a divorce—ones that we dread. As for me, I had to be in the same location as my ex's girlfriend. My son is graduating from 8th grade, and "he" invited her. These three weeks of torture are ones that I never want to repeat. So, why is this still a big issue for me? I guess it's the fact that I've never confronted her—at least in person. So many days had passed by, and each scenario wasn't a good one. However, time does have a way of completing the projects we once set aside. I thought she had a lot of nerve to show up after she had the had an affair with my ex-husband and break up my marriage. On the other hand, I guess I really should thank her. I was in a relationship that hurt my heart as well as my life. I must still deal with "him," but over the past two years, it has gotten easier. I guess I just never wanted to deal with her. Although, all good things must pass when we have to do something we don't want to do.

So, here's the story. That night of graduation, I sat on one side of the room while they sat on the other. I chose my location carefully because I didn't want to be near them. However, one part of the ceremony was where the parents come to the front and light a candle with their child and one of their teachers.

That was awkward! Afterwards, we all gathered for a reception. I was there first, then my ex and his mother, and then "her." After speaking with my ex's mother, "she" showed up and was standing near us. I don't know where my courage came from, but I said hello to "her" and asked how she was! I am not kidding! I did it. She responded with a pleasant comment. Was she as uncomfortable with the situation as I was? Probably, but something made me take charge of the situation—a higher power, perhaps? Whatever it was, all my prior anguish was extinguished in just a few seconds. I also received a comment from a friend at the reception that she was amazed that "he" left me for "that." I believe there was a song that was called, "Things that make you go, Humm!" Of course, the night wasn't all controlled. My ex started another conversation that ticked me off. I guess I'm supposed to roll over and just take it, because he says so! There's a reason I took the "obey" part out of those wedding vows and I have never regretted that decision! I just must keep telling myself, "I can do this" no matter how hard it gets.

# 17.

## The Sun Will Rise Again

With all the advice from friends and family, movies, and new life events, I have learned a lot. Not being together with that person who can make me whole, has given me a time and a place to transform to the person I am today. I have realized what I have, and I appreciate it. For the most part, I have mastered my thoughts and my actions. Then, there are other times where I have no clue what I'm doing. But I have sometimes had to "master" my ex's schemes and stop him in his tracks. Perhaps I'm not ready for the easy things in life to fall into my lap, for the hard times seem so commonplace now.

So, I've found out that life changes and sometimes not for the good. Is this a bad thing? I once thought this way, but I now do not. I really do think that when we obsess about our divorce, it fills up our brain to the point that the word "love" is non-existent. Sounds scary, huh? For, if we look back, has our grieving phase passed—probably not? Has this experience created control issues to the point where we can't shut the door on the horrible tragedy we experienced?

On another note, we have been reminded how love can start out so innocently and we think that it will last forever. For example, I remember attending a wedding since my divorce and I just wanted to say, "I object," when I heard that phrase asking "whom here objects to this union?" I'm glad I kept my mouth shut. It did sound tempting, though. I mean, we all see movies where someone has the nerve to speak up, because we've been there. However, we don't want them to experience nor deter them on the emotions they feel on that day. For, it is the emotions of marital bliss that makes two people happy—right?

I remember when I first took those steps to heal myself; I started going back to church. I remember the minister stating that we must forgive ourselves for tragedies that we have been a part of, for our significant other probably won't. We can't wait on the words, "I'm sorry," from them if they have strayed. Why? I truly believe they feel their actions were justified even though they promised they would never leave us—all in front of a God, a minister, and their friends and family. Now, if we look back, do we regret having married this person? Maybe. Do we regret losing our "family" for someone else's actions? I guess it depends. We may have wanted not to be a family unit anymore; for we dreamed of what it would be like if they were out of our lives. However, it wasn't us who strayed. That regret, or disgust, I really feel will always be there deep down in my heart. We only need to take it out when we feel threatened in a new relationship—or should we? It's like being a child again. We, for the most part, run to our mother and hide behind her skirt tails to avoid pain. I'm right, aren't I?

We cannot wonder what we have missed out on in life since the fairy tale didn't happen to us like we wanted. The life we have now is different, it's not bad, it's not good; it's just different. If we don't have emancipation, life's pitcher will more than likely fill our existence with tears. Life can be sweetened with honey, however, with our outlook from today, all our memories will last until the end of our life. If we have a full cup, it can be filled with happiness—not hate. Sounds like a statement from a sappy movie, huh? Of course it does! Life doesn't allow us to work from Number one to Number nine—in that order. Frustration is what the world is made of and sometimes it drives us crazy. I guess the way the other half of the world reacts to our extremes, is how our day will go. If a mistake is committed and we try to correct the mistake even though we shouldn't even touch it, the reactions of others can send us over the edge.

When we care more about being in a situation (for example, if money plays a big role) than the other person, why are we even there? The effort we put forth goes unnoticed and we feel we are left holding a big fat bag of nothing. On the other hand, it's not just relationships that seem to irritate us. My recent car buying experience just about set me up for a fall. When I bought my brand-new vehicle, a comedy of errors kept happening after the sale. I was mentally ready to lose it. Some people may roll over and let a person or business screw them, but guess what? Not me! I've had this in me for a long time. You know, that attitude that I will win if I know I'm right? I just wish more people, who have gone through a divorce, would follow the advice to not let those "bastards" run all over them. For, if we bottled up our negative feelings, there's nothing but grief just awaiting us down the line.

Here's another bit of advice that I've learned from my fellow divorcees. Examining myself, and the things that are not a part of my life, is important. Who I once was, or how I once acted must be scrutinized—by me. For when a person examines his or her own tragedy and cannot let go of their grief, it saddens me. If we look back, do we really believe who we once were, is not who we are today? Can we be proud of our direction? If you said, "yes" to this question, our past doesn't have to define us now. Or, if we find that love we never had before, do we start all over and marry once again? For, one event can change how we think until we die.

If we can't move forward, is it our deep-down anger that makes us want to punish others—forever? If we suppress our anger repeatedly, will it blow up in our faces? Dealing with it sooner rather than later will help it to not come out like a volcano that can blow up all at once. Because if we don't control our anger, this method of rage will be a destructive and painful event that everyone around you will feel in some form or another. Just remember, wrath is boiled up anger and the root of anger is our hurt. Our unresolved resentment can turn into negative passion. We feel that our hurt can never go away, at least by our hands. Believe me, I've been there, and I was there for a long time. I even saw something on TV concerning how our brain functions when we are so depressed. The frontal and temporal parts of our brain basically shut down and make us unable to function! Are you serious? I am quite serious. Now I know that I'm not totally crazy for what I was feeling.

The conversations that I had with people who said to push my feelings aside and concentrate on work was obviously told to me by someone who didn't understand the human brain! The emotion, the pain, and the hurt can be so great that it clogs us up like hair in a sink drain. It can be so stuck that nothing gets around the emotions, the feelings and any concerns from others, for other people truly don't understand our situation. The power of our life and death situations sometimes comes from the tongue of an innocent bystander who is oblivious to our grief. Don't you think? A person cannot have passion one day and nothing the next day. We can't hide the "stuff" in our closet that hurts us—it will come out eventually, and especially when it hasn't been invited. Dealing with what hurts us will hopefully allow us to not repeat this in the future. I guess the answer lies in what we feel is missing. So, what do we have to chase after to fill us up once again? What do we consider is our "all" in life? There must be an answer.

Just when you think the sun is rising again, there's always someone to throw mud on its glow—either personally or professionally. There are some people in this world who insist upon bullying others to further their self-confidence. Why? Do they feel their sense of authority is threatened if they don't go out of their way to hurt others? I just want to know one thing—where is their sense of security? Has it been misplaced or lost somewhere along life's path? Or do they get some kind of satisfaction hurting others? I've known people like this in a work setting and when they are the boss and this job is your sole support in life, there's not much you can do but document it all and look for a new profession. For, you never know when you must use it against them.

Life will take a turn for all, when you have to prove to HR that you've been wronged.

The world seems so cruel sometimes since we must watch our own back because some people wish to put their foot out to trip us. Besides, the stress we feel everyday is always just a few steps away from our path. In addition, we don't need anyone else added to that grief—but they seem to always be there. So, have we let anger and bitterness in our current life allow us no peace and no rest? Personally, I think we can be our own worst enemy if we don't allow ourselves to relax and not be miserable. Getting God involved in our lives to bring us that much-needed peace, is quite necessary.

As humans, don't we worry too much sometimes? Of course we do! Anxiety in one's heart can cause depression and worry can weigh them down. Then, if we feel more worried because of the "unknown," we take on more worry. Go figure, huh? Then, if we don't have enough to worry about, we seem to make up things to cause us more grief. Hello? Anyone home? I've known people whose minds don't shut down. Say what? Now, there's still no one at home; but, if there is, go back to sleep! If we're concerned about our future, say a prayer to God. Asking him to direct you and your decision will get you further than worrying about the little things you can't control.

If you need guidance, and I believe we all do, start evaluating the results of your prayers. Think of it this way, first it aligns your heart with God. Next, remember that he really will respond with peace to surround your heart. Lastly, you will be protected in every way. So, open the door, and the peace and desire for success will come.

Perhaps we need to re-evaluate our lives and then draw that much-needed map on our next destination? If we don't know where we've been, then how do we determine where we go next? I guess it's like planning a road trip; we need the finances and gasoline to drive to that next town. We also should look, evaluate and take in the view that we've never seen before. For example, if a person has never been to the Grand Canyon, the awe of grandeur is overwhelming. There is so much landscape to take in and digest.

Life can also be so overwhelming. Especially if the rug is pulled out from under us and now, we are left lying on the ground on our backside with no way to rise. At this point in my life, my past is still very much a part of me. To this day, I strive to move forward, and the painful parts of life still sting like a bee. Sometimes I hate my life, but most of the time, I am happy and content. I know I've said it before, but the hurt is still real—will it ever go away?

As time passes, I know each person who has been divorced has looked back at that moment and wondered if marriage was just a contract for our sexual needs. Should we have put up with what we did, just to keep peace? Or should we just have sucked it up and coped in our own way? I guess it depends on your ideals of marriage. I've even heard of "sexless" marriages where each person has their own reason to stay. That's interesting!

Well, I got a revelation this weekend—in church of all places! What I mean is that one man who was an integral part of the church was asked to leave. Apparently, he was pursuing four different married women with flowers and text messages. I've heard some men say that one woman drove them crazy, so why would he want to have a harem surrounding him? Does he have some kind of death wish with that much estrogen in his life? I often wonder about this extremist, far left version of thinking. What goes on today is quite interesting to me. In addition, I now know what the church thinks about morals!

Another message I received today in church is that couples should treat each other with submission and respect. I guess it's like I've always said. If you treat the CEO the same as the janitor, you should never have a problem! Think of dating like this—a new significant other is a person you pursue, but you never really know if they are "the one" for which you're meant to be with forever. The Pastor reiterated that if you were "right with God," this true person would come into your life. I've seen it before and he's right. He also stated that if a person is 100% content being single, then they're ready for marriage. Plus, my opinion is if we don't look for a relationship, it will show up unexpectedly. Strange how that works, huh?

Another thing that I learned which amazes me, and I totally agree with, is that men need respect, and women need to be loved. Also, I've learned that if men don't get the respect from their spouse, they feel they deserve, they would seek out another person to fulfill this need. On the other hand, if a woman doesn't get the love, they need from their partner, the respect they once felt for them is gone. Thus, setting off a chain of events of infidelity for them both. It makes sense, huh? When I heard these words, my eyes were opened wider than ever before. Another way to put it is that men become unloving to their wives if women don't feel loved by them. Also, if one partner feels as if his or her opinion does not matter, a challenge between the two of them begins. Regaining that respect and self-worth is now the goal. However, that disrespect can seep into the relationship, and it may never leave.

Putting focus into a marriage regarding the responsibility of each person will build a stable foundation. Remember each team has a working relationship with the ultimate goal—to be happy and content. The mission of marriage is to be loved and cherished by your partner. Now, for men, here is a word of advice—the secret to loving your wife is quite simple. Ask her the questions for which she

## Attempting To Let Go

desires the answers! It sounds quite simple, but she is the ultimate person who counts, and she actually knows the answer! If you don't understand a person, bitterness can start quite quickly.

The act of expecting something from the other just because they are female, or male is asking for trouble. Men, do you expect dinner to be ready when you get home from work? Even though your wife has a full-time job, makes dinner, takes care of the kids, and does the housework? Or, wives, do you expect your husband to finish that "honey do" list, go shopping with you, and/or fix the car? Do you have a visual now? Do you get the picture?

Expectations are something we sometimes get totally caught up in when we don't think about the other person, especially if they need to be involved. It can pollute your relationship and promote anger from what you expect to happen. You feel disrespected and not appreciated from a broken trust. I know I've been there! These are things that can clog your ability to love that special person. If a relationship is to work, one must obtain a capacity to love. Think about it—if you close out yourself to God, you close off everyone.

I've discussed it before, but it's important to bring it up once again. Now that a lot of time has passed, how are our feelings towards that individual who broke our heart? Especially since this time has passed, are you still bitter about where you are in life now? Have you excelled, while your "ex" has fallen down the well into oblivion, or vice versa? Have you seen you ex and their significant other spiral downward so far that they cannot get back up? Is this the case for you or someone you know? I am now in a situation where certain events have happened, and I don't understand why they're happening.

If I look back years ago, my ex had a belligerent, obnoxious attitude that "no one can touch me," and I truly believe he felt this "high" would always be there. It was not ok with me, but I put up with it. Believe me, I've had my "highs" in life, but I don't think I ever thought I was that much better than anyone else. Money, prestige, and powerful people seemed to fuel this fire. Now the money, friends, and status have gone to his left. Do I feel sorry for him? Do I feel that karma has finally arrived—at least for a short stay? I don't know that answer. But the more I think about his situation, I really feel compassion for him. He has been so highly praised in his lifetime, but now he is financially scraping the bottom of the barrel to exist. It makes my stomach turn to know that a person has to learn life's lessons this way. I'm just so glad that I got my life on track that promotes my son and me. I wanted my own life; not what was left over from where he left me. It was hard at first, but I have created a vision for myself, and I'm very proud of what I have accomplished. "He" had nothing to do with my decisions to be where I am right now. However, I wish him the best; I really do.

I also hope that his eyes have been opened for what others deserve in life—that pain and grief were not on the same menu.

# 18.
# The Final Chapter -- Maybe?

As each day passes, the rise and fall of regular people and celebrities never seems to amaze me. I guess we're all created from the same mold, whether we have money, fame, or fortune. Even Arnold Schwarzenegger, at the time of this book, came out and admitted to an affair around 10 years ago, resulting in a child. Doesn't life understand we've had enough men cheating on their wives? On the other hand, where are the women who cheat on their husbands? I'm not taking up for those men with the Scarlet "A" on their shirt, but why do we not hear about the women? Or are they just better at not getting caught? Good question.

It's an interesting theory that one sex gets their hand caught in the cookie jar, and the other gets away unscathed. Right? Well, maybe not. No matter if you're a man or woman, I know you're reading this passage and thinking that life isn't fair, and you can never trust any partner ever again. Part of this may be true, but it isn't always the case in every situation. There are relationships out there, today, that really work and because there is trust between two people. It's just when there's a "third" person present that all "Hell" breaks loose—tell me I'm wrong! Right now, you're agreeing with me, I just know it. If you've followed me in this series of books, you've seen the hurt that an outsider plays in a relationship. That poison is present, and it tends to seep into every portion of two people's lives, and sometimes a third, when the antidote doesn't exist.

We must find the balance in our lives and then seek out the equilibrium in life's journey. The preparation that our existence gives us allows us to move forward—one foot in front of the other. Each day I keep looking forward to finding those answers that I still struggle with today. I am still scared, and I don't know what lies ahead. But what I do know is that I am more prepared to deal with the complexities of what life throws my way. God is showing me where to go next. That arrow is now more visible, and it is pointing in the approved direction—I just wish it had a brighter neon sign! All I must do is walk that way. It's never easy. I never said that did I? Ha! I just know I should have faith in the man above and in myself. Trust is still coming very slowly back into my life—even after two years. My heart was put through the flames, and all I do is scrape off the burnt parts, because now I'm ok? That's still easier said than done.

Where we are now, we can look back on a journey that we must never forget, and how we arrived at our current destination should be celebrated. We must arrive at a calm and remember to pray for our next move. Past events can never be forgotten, especially when the hurt is still fresh after days, months, and years have passed. Looking at that "horrific" time in one's life can surely taint your view of many people. Our faith must be in a higher power to allow us to forgive those people we now call our "ex," but it still seems to be a challenge. Even our life, after some time has passed, can still be troubled since the love we feel has either been destroyed or polluted. Remember, we must still pursue love in our life; the patience we have in a new relationship can nourish our hope for future events. We can still have joy during times of affliction, however, our faith must be present, for what comes out of our heart is really who we are.

As the days, months, and years have passed, I have realized that actions and words bring clarity in a bond, and also in a breakup. Being on fire in a relationship and then having it extinguished by that person you once relied upon can be very devastating. If that person leaves you, what do we think now? On the other hand, if we break off a relationship that we know isn't working—are we to be blamed forever? Or, if there is reconciliation on the horizon, do we jump on it because we need them, or anyone, so desperately? A marriage takes the efforts of two people wanting it to work. Now, think of a relationship in this manner; if someone does nothing for the relationship to grow, but proclaims their love, is it the same as one who tells of their love and has a hard time showing it? Leaving a question in a person's mind is not the answer. Not knowing why something has happened leaves a blank spot in our brain. For, our mind searches for anything to fill the void, and most of the time it's the worst-case scenario. I don't know about you, but I think it's a recipe for disaster. Don't you think that if a person has a question about their relationship, and it's never asked, how will we ever know the answer? Sometimes the questions we never ask seem to be our demise, huh?

I recently heard a saying that truly struck me. It stated that all endings are new beginnings—we just don't know it at the time. I guess when we finally figure out our life's direction, we're not in charge anymore, or are we? Perhaps yes, perhaps, no. I guess if we hold onto the game of life that our ex handed us when we broke up, our former life will go away, or does it? It's only if we choose to go down that familiar path that it will stay the same. However, we can create the buds of a new life but only if we choose. Whether or not we still love them, their actions and ours have changed the course we were once on. The path has shifted, and we must regroup on how our life and plans will now occur. It's never easy; I'm not saying that it is. It's just the fact that we may not have an obvious strategy unless we keep our eyes on our ultimate reward—our sanity. Our plans may also take us to unknown pastures. Looking back will do us no good. We will only ponder the bad things, but attempting to move ahead can get us one step closer to where we should be in life. One thing that I have learned by writing this series of books is that when you keep falling, you can get up on your own—when no one is looking. You can now feel that you have succeeded in something. I guess it's just like a child who learns to walk. Each time they fall, they may be hurt, but it never deters them from trying again.

My rendition of life is that it can be compared to soap bubbles. They are formed, and they are amazing to look at. However, their life is short, and they can be broken just as quickly as they were formed. I guess the moral of the story is that we should never take for granted what we have; we must embrace it and hold it dear. For, it may not be here tomorrow.

We are given so much in life, but if we don't appreciate it, are we prepared for it to go away just as fast as it was received? For example, relationships with friends and family come and go as the years pass. Some of our friendships can last from elementary school until we die. Others are formed when we become an adult and have an ultimate bond, which can last for a long time, or it can be a passing acquaintance. I guess it's the circumstances and acceptance of having and keeping a connection that we feel we need or don't need. It depends on what we really desire in life that, for the most part, can make our decisions for us. If a part of what we once had is something we still desire, we may or may not go back after it.

Relationships that should have lasted forever, in our mind, may take us back into a U-turn to try and save what may be left. Or, if a relationship was wrong from the beginning, why does anyone still desire it? I've had friends who wanted to dominate our friendship and constantly start fighting with me when we were together. On the other hand, I've had friends that I've never fought with after knowing them for almost 15 years! What gives?

Each new day gives us renewed hope and strength that we never thought we'd ever have again. When the alarm rings to wake us, do we wonder what will happen today? Of course! If it's a Monday, do we look forward to it? Sometimes that answer is "No." For, sometimes, we don't want to move towards a new goal. But isn't it the objective to see the sun rise each day, for we have a new opportunity to change something in our lives that we don't like? I suppose it's all in what we see through our eyes and hear with our ears. We could be sad forever because we "failed," or we could see that we have been given a new chance to correct the mistakes in our life. Don't get me wrong, this isn't a pep talk to make you feel good; it's a conversation between you and your psyche so that you will see life as an opportunity to find a new path.

Every event in life makes us think, "What if things were different, where would I be now." I've done it and I'm sure you have too. So, shouldn't we look at life and realize that with each passing event, we have gotten to where we are now? If we hadn't joined the military, gone to a specific college, or moved to a particular city, how would our lives be different? With each decision we make, we meet new people, accept different jobs, and experience new things that we wouldn't have if we didn't make those decisions, right? Then, all along the way we met people whom we liked and didn't like, dated people we should have never given a second glance, and did things we still regret. With each thing we do, have we prayed for those who rubbed us the wrong way? Say what? I'm serious when I say that those people are the ones who really need our assistance. Prayer bridges the gap between you and others. I guess it is like loving the unlovable. It's hard to ask someone to be kind to those who have hurt you, but forgiveness is the one thing that a person has control over—we just must build up that confidence in ourselves in order to heal.

One thing that I have experienced during my time after the "D" word is that a bad marriage can corrupt one's thoughts and ways. The bitterness we harbor can clog our thinking, our future decisions, and the way we carry ourselves. We must find the light to expel the darkness in our lives. Any relationship is like having a child. You look forward to the upcoming event. Then it arrives on your doorstep. The ups and downs arrive shortly thereafter. Then one day your life changes, and it may never be the same. For, it may take flight and never return to you. If this causes us to not believe in ourselves, we could be kept from doing the things we need to do in our life. For, whatever we focus on can or cannot keep us from bearing the fruit we need to produce. I don't know about you, but I don't desire any part of my past seeping into my future. It's then that we realize that our smile has been broken—now, we just have to find a new one.

I have a friend that I've known for 14 years, and I would never have met her if I hadn't gone back to night school to finish my degree. She has been there for me through so many events and given me her words of advice. She is a friend whom I will always treasure—all due to my decision to acquire my degree! Go figure? Just remember, there are people and events out there for our taking; we just have to have desire in our heart to reach them.

Life's events are sometimes not easy to deal with, but if we don't have an ambition to seek something, we shall NEVER find it. I even find myself coming up with ideas that I would have never thought of while I'm in the shower. I then find myself not writing them down and then I forget what they were. If we don't write down our goals, aren't we more likely to not strive for them? I truly think so because we don't have them available at our fingertips to constantly remind us why we should change direction in midstream to better our lives. If we had a constant reminder why we should do or not do something, don't you think we'd think twice about doing something "stupid" next time? I know I fit into that category! For, have we have learned our lesson in one respect of our day-to-day lives, but then we go back to it? Afterwards, don't our friends want to "beat the living tar out of us?" If we don't believe in ourselves to grow and learn from the things that made us miserable in the first place, where is our brain? Plus, going back to what was comfortable for us is not necessarily a good thing.

Whatever we focus on and then feed on, therein lies the fruit we bear. Whether it is frustration or success, we really do control our destiny; we need to have the stamina to just go for it. I don't know about you, but I don't want my past, that hurt me so desperately, to be repeated in my future. Even though the comfort is familiar, it is not true for me. I guess "brain damage" was meant for some other person?

I have talked a lot about life, family, and those significant others who drive us crazy. From now on, our lives are what we make them. We could allow ourselves to become what we once were, and what we hated about ourselves, but why? We could rely on our friends, our family, or even narcotics to survive, but shouldn't we look back at what got us here first and foremost? I guess what I'm saying is that we each need to analyze what we want out of life, weigh and measure it, and then go for that goal we never thought we could have. It may, again, not be what we should have, but at least we got off our backside and woke up!

On that note I would like to leave you with something a former co-worker told me recently that has stuck with her for a long time. This saying really hits home about what happens in people's lives and where they sometimes go when they can't deal anymore. About 40 years ago, she was in a bathroom and happened to see something written on the wall. She told me she wishes that the author would have signed it, but it was anonymous. Here it is, "Reality is just a crutch for those who can't deal with drugs." Thanks, Betsy—you hit the nail on the head!

## *The End*

## *References*:

Shella Tejada Villamor, Elena, "5 Reasons Why You http://ezinearticles.com

Coontz, Stephanie, "How To Stay Married," (November 30, 2006). Retrieved October 22, 2010. From http://stepahaniecoontz.com

C.C., "Top 25 Reasons to Stay Married." Retrieved October 22, 2010. From: http://scribd.com

Folbre, Nancy, "Dr. Scott's 365 Reasons Why Marriage ROCKS," (Feb 2010). Retrieved October 22, 2010. From http://www.365reasons.com.

Waite, Linda J.; Browning, Don; Doherty William J.; Gallagher, Maggie; Luo, Je; and Stanley, Scott M. "Does Divorce Make People Happy?" Retrieved October 22, 2010. From http://americanvalues.org.

"Colorado Divorce Statistics," Retrieved October 22, 2010. From: http://www.Edivocepapers.com.

Young, Beth. "Why Do You Stay Married?" (2006-2007). Retrieved October 22, 2010 - www.marriageadvice.com. From http://www.prweb.com

Friedman, Marty, "Marriage and Divorce Statistics," Retrieved October 22, 2010. From www.meninmarriage.com

Staff Report. "25 Tips On How To Stay Married," Retrieved October 22, 2010. From http://www.gosanangelo.com

Zodiac Signs Astrology, http://zodiac-signs-astrology.com/zodiac-signs/leo.htm, Retrieved January 14, 2011.

www.ingramcontent.com/pod-product-compliance
Lightning Source LLC
Chambersburg PA
CBHW061757070526
44586CB00023B/2612